Tales of a Gaspipe Officer

Tales of a Gaspipe Officer

With the Cyclists on the Western Front During the
First World War

By "Despatch Rider"

(W. H. L. Watson)

LEONAUR

Tales of a Gaspipe Officer
With the Cyclists on the Western Front During the First World War
by "Despatch Rider"
(W. H. L. Watson)

FIRST EDITION

Leonaur is an imprint of Oakpast Ltd

Copyright in this form © 2021 Oakpast Ltd

ISBN: 978-1-78282-998-0 (hardcover)
ISBN: 978-1-78282-999-7 (softcover)

http://www.leonaur.com

Publisher's Notes

Contents

Cyclists on the Western Front

1. Prologue

The village of St Jans, which is in French Flanders a mile or so from the Belgian Frontier, contains an *estaminet* that, to the best of my remembrance, has no name beyond the proprietor's, and the name of the proprietor cannot be pronounced and is never remembered. This *estaminet* almost faces the well-known *Maison Commune Estaminet* and the huge convent which in February 1915, both before and after, was filled with wounded and sick men and officers, who, for the most part, played good bridge.

In the main room of the nameless *estaminet* were living three officers, Bill, and M'Queen, and Jumbo. M'Queen, who was a captain, commanded the Divisional Cyclist Company. Bill, who was also a captain, and Jumbo, ruled platoons. There was a third platoon with no officer. So the Gaspipe Officer walked down one evening from the top of the hill, reported himself to M'Queen, and, instead of eating, sleeping, and having his being in a tiny room together with five others, found himself an officer and a gentleman with a servant to wait upon him and thirty odd men of his own. . . .

It was a famous company. Before Mons it had pedalled in triumphantly from a successful little affair of outposts. It had waited for the Germans when some squadrons of a famous regiment had ridden through it in despair. Every day and every night of the Great Retreat it had kept unwinking guard on the rear of the division. The men of the company had never tired and had never been driven in. Then the division advanced with the cyclists merrily ahead of it. On the Marne they had rounded up a hundred and fifty German Guardsmen, and brought in eighty, although shelled by their own guns they were then not sixty strong.

On the Aisne they were out every night patrolling a sensitive sector of the line, and, near La Bassée, held as a mobile reserve, they were twice thrown against the German attack, and they stayed the attack. The division went north. Every man was hurled into the firing line for the defence of Ypres. The cyclists were put into the trenches at Hooge, and there they lost their commanding officer, a very gallant gentleman, who, being seriously wounded, passed through hospitals until he came home. And in February 1915 the company was patrolling miles of wire and making innumerable fascines. . .

It was a famous company. Also, it was a comfortable *estaminet*. The new officer nervously drew in his chair to the great blaze of the fire and ordered a drink. He thought without regret of the tiny stuffy room and Grimers laboriously frying a dab over a smoking, evil-smelling stove.

2. Night-Life In Paris

It was M'Queen that raised the point.

"You know, my dear Gaspipe, you were filthy and unshorn. Since you've become an officer, you've made attempts. . . . You have shaved, and, so far as I can see, you are clean. But I really can't have one of my officers going about in the tattered kit of a corporal. We'll try the div."

M'Queen was right. And there was a further difficulty. The callow sub had been a brother-in-arms to the men he was now supposed to command. He had sung choruses to the vile songs of Foster, that very Yorkshireman. He had been given tea at all times, and in all places. Jock, the Company tailor, was an honoured and frequent guest of the Despatch Riders' Mess. Had he not empurpled many an evening? A few days before the cyclists had entertained their future despot to a fine meal and odorous memories of Croucher and his pork chop still lingered. A little leave of absence and a lot of new kit might solve the difficulties of discipline.

The div. was tried and found wanting. No leave and kit to be obtained through ordnance. But the Gaspipe Officer possessed certain physical peculiarities for which ordnance had never allowed.

The idea was Jumbo's.

(Jumbo is a Territorial officer of fabulous girth, energy, and language. He had spent the early days of the war fiercely defending the coast of Yorkshire, and he filled us with such tales of day and night work without rest or food that we all firmly believed the real heroes of this war had never fired a shot except at spying bushes in a doubtful light.)

"Paris is not so far from St Jans. It can be reached by rail or motorcycle. He has a pass and can get a motorcycle. Send him to Paris for his kit!"

The sergeant of the despatch riders, old Huggie, saw the point of the argument and turned a blind eye as the young officer prepared his old motorcycle for a long journey. Then it began to rain, so the man who had been compelled to ride by night and day in every kind of weather sighed for softer methods of journeying.

Finally, Tommy took him to Bailleul in the sidecar. A supply train left for Paris at 6.30 p.m. There was interval for a good dinner and a final toast at the Canon d'Or.

It was strange to wait on Bailleul platform for the Paris train. The guns had ceased their grumbling, for the darkness had fallen and protective day had fled to let loose the night's grim little battles. There is night life beyond Wulverghem, and there is night-life in Paris. That was one of the obvious thoughts that flew into the Gaspipe Officer's head, for a platform beckons obvious thoughts. And the black trucks, like cows in Sussex, stood round patiently, filled with things for those men beyond Wulverghem. . . .

The train officer was kindly but irritable, and he wanted a Mess President; for, though he travelled between Bailleul and Rouen or Boulogne (there are good shops in these towns), he dined off a Maconochie. He also played Bridge, and entertained his fellow-passengers with the complaint that, such were the hardships of his exigent service, he had been unable to obtain more than one rubber or so a week. He had a respect, though, for the combatant, and listened with open mouth to a cyclist and an infantry officer swopping yarns.

The first-class carriage was luxurious. As they dozed the combatants heard the murmur of his voice:

"Simpkins doubled, but we ran out with one to spare. But it's so rarely one gets the opportunity on this rotten job is it very wet in the trenches just now . . .?"

The old supply train jogged on very, very slowly. There were occasional shoutings the seats extraordinarily comfortable.

Amiens! Amiens!

The Gaspipe Officer stood sleepily on the platform, watched the old supply train flounder out of sight, then turned instinctively to the Restaurant. War or no war, it is the *epyov* of Amiens Restaurant to produce good breakfasts and hurried drinks when the Paris Express has a moment to spare. The waiter was old and the cashier was ugly, but the omelette was good.

Once started it is easy to journey from Bailleul to Paris. A train marked PARIS came in, so without further ado he took his seat, and, though the pass he carried did not possess sufficient stamps and signatures to forward a cat from Clapham Junction to Earlsfield, the cyclist officer was not questioned.

There was no getting away from the war. At one place and another neat batteries of seventy-fives were drawn up in green fields, German prisoners, seemingly cheerful, were working in the yards, and dear old Frenchmen, with beards as long as their bayonets, stood impatiently on guard.

The pass proved sufficient to enter Paris, and Paris smelt the same as ever, when the cyclist drove to his favourite hotel in Montparnasse.

At first Paris seemed little different to the Paris he had known. Men in mufti still walked about the streets, and the Taverne Royale was as superlative as it had ever been. So, while his uniform was being made, he went to the correspondent of a famous English daily and to an American artist.

The correspondent said nothing but asked much. The cyclist remembered that he had been a Despatch Rider, and told many tales, of which a few fringed the truth.

The American artist lived in a delectable studio with his sister. They began about the war, talking of those worthy citizens who had fled to Bordeaux and shamefacedly returned; of the true and spurious widows that flocked the boulevards; of life in the trenches and the cause of it all; of Nursing and Art and the high price of food; of the models who were starving in the streets. Then wisely they abandoned war, and led the cyclist through simple pleasures. It was a dream.

Mistily he remembers now the lobster and the artichoke at the Clou an old thin man sang patriotic songs in a cracked voice and everybody laughed with the fine walk back from Montmartre to Montparnasse. No one walks abroad in Paris now late of nights, and Paris is really dark; but the sleepy *gendarmes* smiled at "brav'Tommie," and let him go by.

Then there was the cosmopolitan teaparty with Marice, where French, American, and Roumanian met, and all proved more insular than the Briton. . . .

The dream becomes wilder and stranger, a very proper meal for the fancy of a young officer caged in an exiguous dug-out—afterwards he chewed the memory of Polaire, coldly untamed, chanting a too passionate song. At the Grand Guignol he sat between a corpulent general and a girl in black, each of whom would interpret the jokes confusedly. Add a tiresome walk to see the misty dawn from St Sulpice: the dawn was veiled with clouds, but the breakfast was good.

The maddest scene was the brown interior of a dilapidated cabaret in Montmartre, wherein Marice and her friends were giving a cheap and satisfying meal to artists and models for little or nothing. It was the opening night of the *Cantine des Humoristes*. The walls, covered with obscure drawings, rattled to their laughter. A fat poet sweated well with modest excitement, as in tones of screaming admiration he recited verses that praised vividly the charge of the British Lancers at the Marne. A squat-nosed Russian sang unintelligible ballads that had roaring choruses and somebody's daughter danced.

At the farther end of the room a monstrous wooden crucifix, wonderfully carved, stretched its kind shadow over a humourist and his model, who, replete with mirth and unexpected food, slept smilingly with gaunt faces touching. And through the half-open door, to complete the fantastic show, a crescent moon gazed in over the crenelated roof of a black and ruinous stable.

The dream continued. The cyclist and his friends raced down the steps away from a worthy American girl who was solemnly collecting autographs, and two hospital orderlies of the same tribe, who stood husky with admiration for the British, to a lady that was said to smoke opium, and certainly preferred bull pups to children. She was charming in her pink flannel dressing-gown, but received them with so transparent a hospitality and so cold a kindness that they left her in haste and, talking of the Hippogriff and other famous beasts, walked cheerily over the river to the studio. There they talked theories of art until the day dawned.

The uniform became rapidly ready, but it is easier to enter Paris than to leave her. It was only after interviewing countless railway officials that, coming at last to an ancient and sympathetic staff officer, the magic word "Mons" produced a pass. So, early one morning, Marice as the cyclist's sweetheart, and the American artist and sister as his brother and cousin, were admitted to see the last of the Boulogne Express. . . .

An officer lucky enough after seven months in Flanders to find himself in Paris should make curious investigations into the state of the city and its gains and losses in time of war. It would have been interesting to compare London in December with Paris in February, for surely the observer should be unprejudiced, having seen neither city since the war began. Yet, I ask you, coming to Paris from Bailleul, how could Paris be other than a dream?

Paris seemed less calm and more sensitive than London There was an eager and hourly anxiety it was not fearful but rather a tightly strained interest and the war was not a great shadow to be avoided by pleasuring, or a subject as threadbare as the weather. In Paris a man never says, "What is happening in the war?" or "How are things going on in Flanders?" But rather, with a vivid acceptance of the phrase, "How did we do yesterday?" In London war is an entity outside man's life. It has an objective existence of its own. In Paris the fact and thought of war have become an actual part of life. It definitely flavours everything. London is at war—Paris is in the war.

Yet in some ways Paris has become curiously British. In February, the Parisians were ceasing to wonder at, and were beginning to understand, London's "More pleasure than ever." *La Vie Parisienne* and more important journals were beginning to joke at London's assumption of the traditional French gaiety and the Parisians' assumption of the traditional London sobriety. So, though the artists were starving—*Bal Bullier* is a barracks and *Colorossi's* is shut—Paris awoke like a tired woman and wearily made herself gay.

And Paris vies with London in its suppression of enthusiasm. The cyclist stood in front of the Madeleine and watched a battalion swing down the boulevards and into the Rue Royale. There was no cheering—only a rare self-ashamed shout, for this war is not a gasconading enterprise. In France, when sons or fathers go to the war they are not heard of for months and months. So the parade of soldiers is to many the parade of ghosts. . . .

The Express came to Boulogne late in the afternoon. The journey had not been dull, for the train was filled with American correspondents and French staff officers in their horizon blue uniforms, who chattered with interest at the sight of prisoners and war material, or when the train barely crept over a newly repaired bridge. At lunch a friendly captain sat opposite the cyclist, told him what was happening down Festubert way, and invited him to proceed from Boulogne in the car of a friendly interpreter.

Boulogne was unsatisfactory, as it always is in war-time, for Boulogne is neither Home nor Front. It overflows with ambulance drivers, and strayed officers, and men of mark in the I. M.S., who seem without work, and delicious nurses in delectable oilskins who flock the tea-shops and gladden the heart and eyes of a returning officer. Going on leave—Boulogne is only a place in which the bus or train stops a few hundred yards from the ship.

To the wounded it may be a hellish or heavenly caravanserai, as the wound is light or serious a purgatory for the convalescent on light duty, a space surrounding a board of officers who determine whether you may or may not be granted sick-leave at home.

The cyclist and his friend, the captain from Festubert, determinedly looked for the brighter side of Boulogne, and went near to finding it. Tea was at a teashop filled with I. M.S. and nurses. Then the interpreter and car arrived and they went to dinner, but outside the restaurant the cyclist had seen a staff car of his own division. This proved to be important, because there was little or no room for the cyclist in the interpreter's car. An artist, fat, and with a certain enthusiasm, had come to Boulogne, and desired to paint battles at Armentières—a simple wish. He was a friend of the interpreter, and the interpreter was stationed at Armentières.

So, the cyclist went in search of the staff car and found Grimers, who with his usual tenacious pursuit after pleasure, had come into Boulogne on the car to buy fish for the despatch riders. Just after dawn—it was bitterly cold—the car called for the Gaspipe Officer. It was tricky driving, because the roads were frozen and the tyres were steel-studded. At St Omer they learned that Grimers had been given a commission, and beyond Cassel they knew certainly that the Canadian Division had arrived, because its immense green transport was woefully in the way.

Before Caestre the clutch began to slip, and finally in front of that white farm where the divisional train used to make its headquarters half way between Bailleul and St Jans the engine that had been doing much work with no result found it could not heave the car out of a rut. So, the cyclist took up his baggage and walked.

In the main room of the *estaminet* Bill, Jumbo, and M'Queen sat over the fire in earnest consultation. When he entered M'Queen looked relieved, and, smiling uneasily, said

"Glad you're back; thought the division was beginning to smell a rat. Anyway, we've got some excellent news to welcome you home with."

"What's up?"

"The cyclists," he read, "will take their turn with the divisional cavalry in garrisoning the trenches."

Jumbo, for no reason at all, roared with laughter.

3. Night-Life Beyond Wulverghem

It is no joke at all for cyclists to be put in the trenches; trenchcraft cannot be learnt in a night. Cyclists have neither the knowledge, the experience, nor the appliances. Jumbo laughed, because, for many strenuous years a Territorial and for many packed mouths on home defence, he was at last to see real war. He talked boldly of listening-posts and crawling up to the German wire, but the Gaspipe Officer was filled with dread.

The despatch riders whom he had left jeered at him, and pointed out it was argument unanswerable that the coming together of the trenches, his ignorance, and his physical eccentricities, would result in certain death. George said it was a shame. To put the Gaspipe in the trenches was simply to make a present of a might-be valuable officer to Fritz or Hans, or whomsoever the sniper of the day might be.

The cause of it all had occurred further up the Line. A division composed of foreign service battalions had arrived and taken over from the French. This division was handicapped in many ways. First, a man who has been stationed at Hong-Kong, and then for a month or two at Winchester, cannot feel marvellously comfortable in Flemish trenches during a wet spring, even if his health does not actually suffer. Second, the trenches which this division took over were, I am told, downright bad trenches. The Germans, knowing all this, attacked vigorously.

So, two of our war-worn brigades were sent up north to restore the balance of power. This they did effectively and quickly; but in the meantime, two very weak brigades came south to hold our sector of the line, which was comparatively quiet. They were so weak that the cyclists had to go to their rescue.

Now the trenches of Flanders are known almost as well as the hotels. The Faucon and the Canon d'or are familiar to many. So is trench 10*b* Support. It is still, I believe, a comfortable and satisfactory trench. It was in February last and the cyclists rejoiced when they were bidden to garrison this trench and 10*a*, another quite healthy ditch. The trenches themselves were safe. Casualties usually occurred going in or coming out.

The divisional cavalry, who were sportsmen, took the first shift, and lost enough men to make their major tear his hair, for valuable N.C.O.'s trained in the work of divisional cavalry are not easy to replace. . . .

The evening came. M'Queen and the Gaspipe, cheered by a supper of champagne and oysters for who can make a better Mess President than an ex-despatch rider? embarked on waggons with half the company, and slowly trundled along on bad and desolate roads towards the trenches. It was not raining, but the air was chill and dank. Dranoutre, never a cheerful village, looked like a melancholy dog that had come out of the water but forgotten to shake itself. The shattered trees cast dreary shadows. The men, who had been singing, became quiet and whispered among themselves.

Behind a slight, purple ridge ahead of them the pistol-lights were whizzing up and rifles crackled almost merrily. They disembarked near a little *estaminet*, and, while the men took their tea from a borrowed field kitchen, M'Queen and the Gaspipe swilled down many cups of *café-cognac*, admired the baby, and endeavoured to understand how many brothers, sons, and fathers of our hostess were serving. There was a filthy old man there, too, who cheered us by recounting the feats of German snipers.

At length they started off M'Queen leading and the Gaspipe bringing up the rear. They crossed the top of the ridge and marched down a path which is marked on the map as being open to the enemy's fire. A few "overs" whirred harmlessly by and the cyclists felt almost brave.

Now, although the cyclists were quite convinced that the Germans were filled only with the thought that the cyclists were coming, the facts were that there were other troops also on the road and that it was very dark. The Gaspipe halted his platoon in the rear of some shadowy figures, and only after some minutes discovered that these figures had nothing to do with him.

So he hurried on and caught up M'Queen in the main street of a ruinous village. There M'Queen told the men what to do. They were not to be frightened of stray bullets and duck. They were to bury their faces in the mud when the lights went up. It was easy to talk, but the village rustled uneasily with the *zeep-zeep-ping* of the bullets and multitudinous little crashes as they flew through the broken walls.

"I doan't loike this—place," murmured a man from Suffolk, and one officer at least agreed with him.

Again, they forged on along a winding and slippery path. The *zeeping* grew more furious, and the Gaspipe, ducking his head to one that seemed viciously near, hoped that the darkness covered his sin and endeavoured to believe the obvious, you cannot hear the bullet which hits you. So, they stumbled forward, and having passed the stretch in which the cavalry had suffered, grew more cheerful.

At last a weary—"Halt. Wait here. It's dead ground."

It was dead ground—a flattish slope of black mud pock-marked with shell holes and lined with tiny streams. On either side were little groups of withered trees and bushes. Over the ridge were much light and noise—for all the world like Port Meadow Fair before you cross the bridge. Instead of the shouting and the music of the merry-go-rounds you heard the uproar of the rifles and the machineguns. And the lights threw a sickly yellow glare upon every tree and bush and man.

M'Queen returned and led the way—planks over streams, round shell holes, and finally into a muddy ditch which was crowded with men. This was 10*b* Support.

"Here's your dug-out," said the officer in charge hurriedly, eager to get away. "It's rather damp, but quite cushy. I've left some bread and *pâté-de-foie-gras*. There's plenty of room for the men. The guardroom is here, and this is where you put your sentries. That's all—oh, one moment. There's a live shell just behind the parados. Don't tickle it—and Fritz enfilades this trench at a height of about 5 ft. 4 in. That's him! Keep down. Goodnight."

Thus, the Gaspipe Officer was left in charge of 10*b* Support. He gave a few hurried orders, crawled into his dug-out, and determined to stop there until he was relieved. He disliked Fritz intensely.

The dug-out was constructed, like most dug-outs, of sandbags filled in with Flanders mud which is a bad imitation of clay. The floor was of beaten earth. The length of it was five feet, the width three, and the height about two. Every inch of it was dripping, but inside a sleeping sack spread on the top of a groundsheet life was tolerable, though no arrangement could keep the dripping off the face.

He had just snuggled into the sleeping-sack when a *chit* was brought from M'Queen—"Come and look me up."

He slid out of the dug-out with a curse, and, climbing wearily over a gap in the parados, was led by a friendly corporal to 10*a*, where the cyclists supported by a machine-gun section of Queen Vic's were engaged in what M'Queen called "obtaining a moral superiority over the Huns." Going back to his own trench, the Gaspipe slipped into a shell-hole, and he was very damp when he reached the comfort and shelter of his own dug-out. . . .

He slept soundly, and was wakened at dawn with the report that all was quiet along our front. It was a fine morning after the rain, and the birds sang cheerily. So here was he, a microscopic entity, in charge of one of those trenches, which stretch, as everybody knows, from the North Sea to Switzerland. Behind him was the dark hill covered sparsely with derelict trees. Eighty yards in front—you could see them safely through a certain loophole—were low-lying yellowish mounds faced with odd bits of wire and little heaps of grey.

These were the German trenches—and the fact was not

thrilling. Very occasionally rifles were fired: you would have thought they were fired at random if you had not listened to the ping of Fritz's bullet down the trench. And in the afternoon a few shells screamed like sea-gulls overhead.

So, the troubled night came again. About eleven there were several sharp bursts of fire. The Gaspipe Officer grasped his revolver and wondered how on earth he was going to reinforce 10*a*. He would be quite certain to fall into something on the way there. Before those Great Pushes that occur with such a lamentable frequency men do reach a high enthusiasm (it is given for the balancing of an enormous and immediate death), but down "on the range," even when the surroundings are unfamiliar, the little emotions of nervousness, not fear, and miserableness, not misery, and a wee helping fellow called humour, creep into the dug-outs. The worst of war is that it is so rarely heroic. There are so few occasions which inspire a man to write a really fine letter.

M'Queen in 10*a* had never needed the help of the troubled officer in 10*b* Support. The "moral superiority" had been gained at the cost of much ammunition, and the Germans were aware to look at the matter fairly and squarely that new and green troops were in the trench opposite them. Besides, M'Queen had a telephone and knew everything that was going on up and down and behind the line. He also had a machine-gun.

The morning broke to a gorgeous day. Even the walls of the dug-out dripped less rapidly, and high in the heavens a lark sang with full glory. The German gunners began to try and hit Neuve Eglise, and the British artillery, longing for some excuse to unlock their stores of ammunition, determined to strafe the Germans' trenches and some villages behind the German line.

The show began about half-past eleven with big guns, little guns, and all sorts of guns. Even "Granny," a howitzer quite as effective as any German, let out with one of her elephantine shells, which chortled through the air like an express passing through a tunnel beneath you, and brought down a church with everything near it.

The field-guns banged and whizzed away at the trenches in

front; it was a display more frightful than effective, for shrapnel burst on percussion does not do any great damage even to badly-constructed trenches. The Germans replied mildly with some shrapnel that burst two hundred yards beyond 10*b* Support. No one, except the Germans, knew exactly for what it was meant. Certainly, no harm was done.

When the morning's shelling was over, one of our aeroplanes flew along the trenches to inspect the result. The Germans were so intent on firing at it that M'Queen and his men, disregarding the aeroplane, fired at the Germans. One of the cyclists reported that a second after firing he had heard a German scream.

The Gaspipe Officer had been told that the work of him who is in charge of a support trench consists in keeping man and trench fit and dry. The man was the difficulty. The bottom of the trench was covered with nine inches of water, so planks raised on little piers had been laid along it and just above the surface of the water. The men, disregarding his advice and example, considered trench-life a huge joke, and gallivanting along the greasy boards, splashed splendidly into the water.

Again, everybody knows that to get out of a Wulverghem trench in broad daylight and walk about behind it is to challenge a remarkably swift death. Yet two of his men did it and survived. Truly, the life of the cyclist is charmed!

To keep the trench dry and fit was not a difficulty, because it was impossible. A little digging might have been done: in fact, it ought to have been done. But he had only once before been to the trenches—a fearful night, on which he had volunteered to help lay a wire, or rather watch a wire being laid from battalion headquarters to a fire-trench—and he knew so little about trenches that he dared not make a change. He might disturb something that had a name and was very useful. To exhume a gabion would be indeed a crime. . . .

So, the afternoon wore on, and the evening came when he was to be relieved by the eager Jumbo—and his courage failed him. Jumbo would not sit in a dug-out all the time. Jumbo would dig a new trench after he had improved the old. Jumbo would wander fearlessly up and down the slippery plank, careless of Fritz's cupronickel jibes, and hurl foul language at the Hun. For the rest of time Jumbo would be the warrior and the Gaspipe the craven in the hearts and mouths of the company.

It was now quite dark, and still Jumbo did not come. Reliefs are always too late for the relieved and too early for the reliever: it is a curious temporal axiom. At last a message arrived from M'Queen:—

> Leave your men in charge of Ray and wait for me at the solitary tree.

He scrambled with care through a gap in the parados, and slipping hastily over the black mud, walked with light heart to the solitary tree. The night was pitch-black. There was a low murmur of voices and the *slop-slup* of men marching over the mud. Then a pistol-light would flare up and the dead ground appear alive with black, stumbling files of men, some burdened with rations and water-bottles, some carrying loaded stretchers, some halted waiting to be guided in, and others tired but joyful coming out, very softly whistling.

Soon a little party marched smartly up to the solitary tree—the remaining half-company with Jumbo and Bill, Jumbo almost silent and tense. Soon they left, going trenchwards, and again the Gaspipe waited. The Devil's Fair it was—with its light and music—for sometime those low-lying yellowish mounds must be shattered to destruction by our guns, while the crowded men wait in 10*b* Support and 10*a*, and rush in a great charge. That will be but the beginning, for behind the German trenches a falsely gentle slope rises to the ridge of Messines.

M'Queen came along with his men, and together they tramped to the ruinous village. The path was quiet that night. Quite comfortably they reached the top of the hill and embarked on their borrowed waggons. It was bitterly cold, and they were delayed by an ambulance which could not be passed until they came to a soft place where the ambulance might draw aside easily; but the men, led by Jock the Tailor, sang all the songs they knew, beginning with the more innocent and finishing with the more crude. By the time they had reached the turning to Croix de Poperinghe all was silent except for a muffled curse at the cold. Four hours in a G.S. waggon on a freezing night is no pleasing journey.

The men were dismissed. M'Queen and the Gaspipe hurried to the nameless *estaminet*, where the inimitable Bland had a roaring fire going and a long and steaming dinner. . . .

When Jumbo returned three days later, the Gaspipe waited for an epic narrative, but Jumbo was short in his reply:—

"Eh? I just lay close in that darned dug-out until somebody relieved me."

4. Quiet Times

So, they came out of the trenches with no casualties save a few frost-bitten feet, and wrote home the most amazing letters of their prowess. Without doubt the cyclists had made a noise.

The company, content with itself, slid into a peaceful routine of play and work.

About a quarter to eight the Gaspipe Officer would be called, but getting up was difficult, because, after nights on the more repellent surfaces, a soft bed in a little cosy bedroom above the *Maison Commune* held out the most deliciously retaining hand. Breakfast and a pipe brought him to nine or a quarter past, at which hour Bill, with attendant subalterns M'Queen had left them to buy eggs for a general would walk briskly up to the company's farm, dispense justice and sign multitudinous papers. After censoring the letters a weary job, they would stroll round the country and watch the men making fascines, and so back to letters, papers, and lunch.

Later the order came from the division for the company to take a "refresher" course of training, and the morning would be spent in learning all the things a cyclist must know—to read a map, to fall off his cycle in the twinkling of an eye, to lay traps for cavalry, and to look like a company when riding and not like the Purley Pedallers. Some of these things the Gaspipe taught his men, but most of them he learnt from Bill and his platoon and the sergeant-major. On a pleasant morning, under the instruction of the sergeant-major, he would endeavour to shout orders across the greatest possible number of fields.

After lunch they might stroll into Bailleul or play football. Bailleul was never quite dull. In the spring territorial divisions began to arrive, and the Gaspipe with Jumbo or Bill used to saunter up and down the square and criticise with a veteran air. A division in column of route—the guns and limbered waggons rattling and groaning over the cobbles: the men grinning with happiness, for to many Bailleul was almost "the Front." Never will the cyclists forget "Tango the Lion-Tamer," an officer who, to the pure joy of all the civilian and military inhabitants of Bailleul, appeared in a leopard-skin coat. Everybody asked everybody else:—"Have you seen Tango?"

From the square they would saunter into the dirty and smoky Faucon or the expensive Allies Tea Rooms for a drink. The more companionable *estaminets* were closed to officers, the Gaspipe found to his infinite sorrow. There was a little tavern that hung on to the side of the Hôtel de Ville, where Chloe gently provided grenadines and made the most charming compliments to the brave corporals—and another down a narrow wynd not far from old Divisional Headquarters and much frequented by the London Scottish while they were in Bailleul. When these were full of men, it was difficult for a young officer, too sensible of his dignity, to enter.

Later a cinema was provided, while the North Irish Horse, finding life dull after their old freebooting days, started again the fine old sport of cock-fighting. . . .

About three afternoons a week the cyclists turned out to smash their opponents on the football ground. The 3rd Divisional Cyclists were their great rivals; but the matches with the A.S.C. roused the bitterest feeling, for they played too professional a game. Bill excelled on the wing, and M'Queen's masculine coaching was beautiful to hear.

Even in those quiet days of March life was not all such pleasuring. There were wire patrols. The Gaspipe would borrow a motorcycle and ride out to Neuve Eglise or Kemmel way. Then he would walk for miles, following a wire across fields that had been stirred with shells like porridge with a spoon; or down near Wulverghem, or up from the ruins of Kemmel village to the top of Kemmel Hill—and see that his men were doing their work.

It was laborious, unexciting, and infinitely melancholy. A dead and shattered man is a little horrible and almost unimportant, a thing defective, without soul, but dead and shattered country seems always to be suffering dumbly, as though it were a kindly beast in pain. And still it listens each night to the loud reports of the rifles and the whisper of the bullets as they fly complaining over the black and slippery mud. . . .

The rumour came that the division was to move northwards to Ypres. Men freely cursed. The old Ypres salient was such a silly thing. Imagine for a moment one of those old Greek theatres, semi-circular. All the way round the Germans were on the top row of seats, and we were only half-way up. They could see everything that we were doing, while we, hemmed in, had to trust to aeroplanes. And down on the floor of the theatre stood Ypres, through which or by which nearly every road to the salient passed. It is not wonderful that the Germans shelled Ypres. It is amazing that they did not shell it more.

Jumbo went ahead to find billets, and we followed, trekking over Mont Noir—you can see from the smoke of Funes almost to Warneton, and from the towers of Ypres away to Sailly—and through Reninghelst to Poperinghe. There Bill was billeted on a "Wipers Widow" (a refugee lady whose husband still lives in Ypres), Jumbo on a priest, and the Gaspipe on a coal merchant whose brother was still "over there."

In those days Poperinghe was a pleasant city, containing all that the heart of an officer could desire—good grocers, an excellent restaurant or two, and a delectable tearoom. The inhabitants, like all Belgians, are friendly to the point of embarrassment. The children sing "Tipperary" in the streets morning, noon, and night.

Coming in late one night the Gaspipe found the coal merchant urgent for a talk. First, they discussed the price of coal, and the excellent system the British had of bringing their own fuel with them; then, as always happens, they started on the war, and the Gaspipe enlarged mightily on the merits of the voluntary system of enlistment. Finally, the coal merchant described how the Germans had left, and the French and British arrived.

The last to leave were the German cyclists. We all kept sullenly within our houses, for the good God alone knew what the Germans might perpetrate in their defeat. The Germans left, except for one officer, and he rode round the town, firing at all of us, daring any one to touch him, for the Germans always returned. He was a brave man, and we, though we cursed and moved first forward a little and then back, did not dare. The women besought us to leave him alone for fear something should happen to them.

Half an hour later the French cyclists rode through very quickly, then for many hours we were in suspense. There was much noise of cannon, but no one appeared. We opened our doors and flocked into our streets, talking anxiously.

Towards evening the rumour flew round that the English were marching into Poperinghe. We ran to the street by which they were coming and waited. When they came, fine and brave men, we could not cheer for laughing, or laugh for cheering. Such funny little petticoats they wore—

Here the Gaspipe began hastily to talk of other things, for he knew the battalion and what had happened to them, and did not choose to laugh at their kilts. . . .

Bill, Jumbo, and the Gaspipe were comfortable enough in Poperinghe. A little training would be done in the mornings for the sake of appearances, and in the afternoons, they would walk out of the town to have tea with some friends in an ammunition column, or watch the aeroplanes go up. They were, in fact, beginning to realise with shame that they might have belonged to the least combatant branch of the service, when the order came to shift into huts near Ouderdom.

They were well-constructed huts, because the sappers had built them for themselves. You may curse the work the sapper does for other people; nobody, however churlish he may be, can do anything but wonder when sapper works for sapper. There was even a large bath. . . .

5. A Famous Victory and Dirty Work at Ypres

M'Queen came in with the news one morning.

"That sapper fellow tells me we're mining a hill—enormously important place—Germans can see all over the place from it. The show is going to take place at 7 sharp tomorrow evening. The hill's on our bit of the line."

The air was full of excitement. Even the gang of Belgian labourers that worked on the road outside the camp grinned, because they had heard the rumour of an attack. And in the tea-shops of Poperinghe everybody was talking about the mine and the attack after its explosion. A sergeant of the cyclists heard exhaustive and accurate details from an old market-woman. The British officer is not expert in the keeping of secrets.

On the appointed evening the roofs of the huts in the cyclist camp were crowded. The officers standing on a little rise swept the high country beyond Dickebusch with their field glasses and looked often at their watches. At seven Jumbo swore he heard a dull thud. Two minutes later the guns spoke, hesitated, then broke out into an enormous fury of sound. Flash answered flash right along the horizon. The little black group of officers—it was deep dusk—watched the bursting shrapnel narrowly.

"That fellow's a bit high—'m, they're putting a few into old Wipers—a nice old salvo—put it into them, lads—give 'em hell!"

So, they watched the bestial struggle for Hill 60 from Ouderdom, three and a half miles away, half joyful and half sick at heart. Not one of them would have confessed (it would have been mere sentiment), yet each had a great pride in the old div., and a great anxiety that it should do well. Had the charge been successful? Had the gains been consolidated? They went back into their hut and sang any amount of music hall trash until it was time to go to bed.

In the morning news came that the position had been rushed with slight loss; the Germans had been filled with such panic that they had fled from the trenches on either side of the crater: the Germans were heavily attacking: their guns and bombs were sweeping our new position: there was no wire down yet.

About nine the same night there was much cheering in the darkness of the camp. The remains of two battalions had returned from the hill. Then first were learnt the names of the fallen. Still there was no wire down.

At one place we had fought our way to the topmost seats in the theatre, but the cost of it was pitiful. It took five or six days before the wire was down and trenches properly made. During those days no battalion could remain for more than fifteen hours on the hill, and at the end of its shift it would return broken. The men could see the guns that were firing at them.

On the fifth day the Gaspipe was wakened very early.

"The captain says dress at once and go and get instructions from him." It appeared that by luck or design the Germans had dropped a large shell, or more than one, on a certain street in Ypres and blocked it, with the result that many motor ambulances and some regimental transport had been shelled outside the city gate. The cyclists were called upon to clear the street and keep it clear. They must ride to Ypres at full speed.

They started off, and the Gaspipe, to drown the thought that the unblocking of streets under shell fire was no job for a quiet fellow, rode as he had never ridden before. He flashed through Vlamertinghe, and faster and faster along the magnificent macadam into Ypres. Just inside the city the Gaspipe threw himself off his bicycle, breathless, and looked round. There were only two men with him, and nobody else in sight! At that moment he learned definitely that to bring along a platoon or company of cyclists at high speed is a fine art.

Leaving his corporal to form up the platoon as they came in, he rode to report. The town *commandant*, who was comfortably at breakfast, knew nothing about him, but believed that the idea of keeping the street clear was quite excellent. There did not seem to be any urgent need for the services of the cyclists. The vivid picture which the Gaspipe had formed of monstrous labours in deadly danger and a cloud of dust disappeared. Ypres was quiet. He led his men to the Church of St Martin, and went forward to look round.

Beyond the church, an ugly red-brick building hitherto untouched, and a hundred yards or so inside the Lille Gate, there was a narrowing of the road. By craft or luck, the German gunners had thrown a shell exactly on this spot, brought down the houses on either side and blocked the road. Some other cyclists had worked right through the night to clear the street: it was the Gaspipe's job to keep it clear. The cycles were brought under shelter of the broad ramparts, and sentries were posted with orders instantly to report, if still alive, when shells fell near the objects of their solicitude.

Ypres was being shelled very lazily with big stuff, but nothing came near.

Bill and Jumbo arrived in an hour or so, and, like the Gaspipe, were bravely wishing for excitement. They first strolled up the street for a drink. Something dashed across the street just in front of the Gaspipe, and went with a crash through the door of a butcher's shop. For a wild moment the Gaspipe thought it must have been a great cat—until the butcher noisily and triumphantly produced the fuse-cap of a German shell. They walked a little farther, then returned to the walls, where for the first time they experimented with chewing-gum, and disliked it.

It was pleasant on the walls, looking towards Zillebeke over the moat. They form a wide grass covered mound sloping gently to the water. Trenches have been cut into them and dug-outs burrowed. On the other side of the moat, which by the Lille Gate is as broad as a lake, runs the infamous Sunken Road. Last October, when Ypres was being shelled very heavily, troops used to prefer the Sunken Road to a march through the city. This the Germans discovered, and the road became a slaughterhouse. The cyclists knew it, for they had walked along it to the trenches of Hooge.

A couple of miles or more away the sky met a range of low and partly-wooded hills, on which the Germans live. They look down from them on to the dwellers in the plain, and because they can see and not be seen, dwell in a malign and abominable security. . . .

Before the war the old walls of Ypres swarmed on Sundays with burghers and their families in their best. I have always sympathised with fortresses that have become sights for the vulgar, and walls a public promenade. But the veteran ramparts, grown over and neglected, have revenged themselves on time, and, sighing for charge and affray, the creak of the cross bow, and the hearty shouts of the bluff old warfare, have seen and heard such poor multitudes scientifically killed, that again they must be wearying for the gay Sunday quietude. . . .

They had tea in the *atelier* of a dressmaker, and then, having vainly searched their quarter of the town for a worthy drink, packed up their traps and cycled home to Ouderdom in the growing dusk. A guard was left to warn them if again the Germans should block that very important street to the Lille Gate.

All this time there had been bestial fighting on Hill 60. No battalion could remain on the cursed pile of dirt thrown out from a cutting for more than a day and a night. The Hill was death. But the Fifth Division has never let go, and never will. They stuck to the Hill while the sappers put up wire and made it defensible. Everybody had thought we had bitten off more than we could chew, but as nobody said it, we chewed.

So, the spring came.

6. The Afternoon of the Twenty-Second

Butcher, the new subaltern, arrived early in the afternoon with a draft for the company. The Gaspipe took him round and showed him the camp and the more important landmarks, Dickebusch Church, the towers of Ypres, the German ridge, and roughly where the Line was. Butcher was duly thrilled, and said a little sadly—

"Nothing doing just now, I suppose?"

"Nothing much. We lost a horrible lot of men taking a hill during the last week, but things should settle down now for some time. There's talk of a push, but then there always is. Still, there's a show this afternoon—French talking to what's left of the brigade that took the hill."

The brigade, the old 13th, was drawn up in a square. Each battalion was about the size of a weakish company. The general came and told them simply that they were heroes—haggard, laughing men, who, glowing with pride, would afterwards joke about that "damned nuisance, the inspection." And the Gaspipe wondered bitterly how long he would remain to see the 13th again and again destroyed.

In that maimed brigade there were, I think, about four officers and sixty men left of those who had come out in August; but the 13th was still a brigade that could be trusted, a brigade of steady and reliable battalions.

Just after the general had left, an aeroplane descended hurriedly on the parade-ground with a despatch. There was much consultation, and then a car started off at full speed. It was about four o'clock in the afternoon of the twenty-second of April.

Bill and Jumbo went into Poperinghe. The Gaspipe and

Butcher strolled lazily towards Vlamertinghe.

"Look there, Gaspipe," said Butcher; "look at those flares going up away to the north. You told me if flares went up before dusk it was a sign of nervous troops. Well, they're durned nervous over there, because it's still quite light. Some cannonade you get, too, every evening."

The Gaspipe looked to the north. Flares were following each other in rapid succession, and the cannonade was become furious. Frankly, he was puzzled.

"I don't understand it," he replied reflectively. "It might be those Canadians who have just taken over from the French, but it's a bit too far north—and I didn't realise that the salient (the Ypres salient, you know) came round quite so far to the west. And, by G—d, listen to that!"

Butcher strained his ears and heard, above the noise of the traffic and shouts and laughter of the men, a swishing, thrilling, crackling sound. Suddenly it reached a sharper note. Beyond Vlamertinghe a vast tree of greasy black smoke appeared, and almost at once a great *bo-boom* reverberated over the fields.

"That's a 'Jack Johnson, G.S., Tommy Atkins, for the use of,'" murmured the Gaspipe, "and what on earth's it doing over there? The Huns are getting uppish. Here are some of my men."

Half a dozen cyclists were riding in rapidly. They had just been relieved from duty on the important street at Ypres. The Gaspipe stopped them.

"Anything up?"

"Yes, sir." The man spoke with an anxious importance. "They've put some mighty big stuff into Ypréss, and, as we was coming back we saw a lot of Frenchies with some transport and limbers, and Jim 'ere thought 'e saw a gun—they was tearing like mad across the fields to Vlamertingy."

"What's up?" said Butcher, when the men had been dismissed to their tea.

The Gaspipe thought a moment.

"Huns fed up with losing Hill 60, and bored with the Canadians, look for trouble—start shelling Canadians and plumping a few behind the lines—hit Belgian working-party—rapid and amazed flight of same. Let's go and get some dinner. Rotten place, Ypres, though!"

They went back to their hut, and, after waiting some time for Bill and Jumbo, started dinner. The cannonade to the north grew louder and nearer. The Gaspipe was not satisfied with his own explanation. Butcher became excited and hoped that something would happen.

It was nine o'clock when Bill and Jumbo came in. Bill was a trifle pale, and Jumbo looked uneasy.

"Any news?"

"Any news! The Germans have broken through between the French and the Canadians! French transport, refugees, and infantry are pouring into Poperinghe from Elverdinghe! Huggie says the road is blocked for miles!"

The heart of the Gaspipe beat with enormous rapidity, and his knees seemed suddenly very weak. He tried to pull himself together. "If the Huns have broken right through," he said with a too admirable calm, "this old division is nicely cut off with one or two others, and there'll be some very pretty rearguard work on hand. You've struck oil fairly early, Butcher."

Bill gave orders for the company to stand to arms and everything to be packed up. Then they sat down to dinner, discussing the situation in detail.

It seemed queer to Butcher that a German break-through three or four divisions up the Line should affect the Fifth Division so vitally. The Gaspipe expounded with the aid of the rough diagram on next page.

The Germans are reported to have broken through at XX, and to be pushing on towards Elverdinghe. Between XX and the Fifth Division the line is held by the 28th, the 27th, and the Canadians. If the Germans push forward to the line O O, the left of the Canadians will be badly in the air. Again, the line P-VL-Y is the road along which all supplies are sent up to the divisions holding the salient. The German occupation of the line O O would literally threaten the British communications. Lastly, behind the line there are very few troops and very many valuable stores and staff officers. . . .

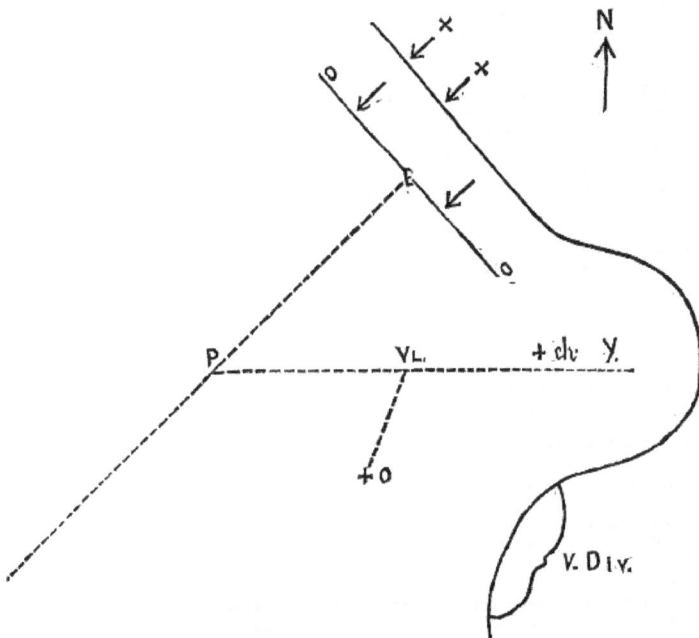

Y = Ypres.   E = Elverdinghe.   P = Poperinghe.   VL = Vlamertinghe.   O = Ouderdom.

Note.— The eccentricities of the line are exaggerated for the sake of clearness.

The sergeant-major brought in a despatch. Two patrols, each consisting of an officer and six men, were to report immediately at Advanced Divisional Headquarters, which were residing at a *château* (ch on diagram) a couple of miles out of Ypres, on the Vlamertinghe road.

In five minutes, Jumbo and the Gaspipe were ready to start. Back tyres were blown up; kit was tied on firmly; rifles were inspected. Jumbo shouted the order—

"Prepare to mount! Mount!"

7. The Night of the Twenty-Second

The road to Vlamertinghe was almost clear. In front of an estaminet on the left of the road "Granny" and her train were drawn up for the night, monster masses of black tarpaulins. On from Vlamertinghe the road was a thick cursing crowd. For some obscure reason we never seem able properly to control the refugees from a bombarded town. It was hugely important to keep clear the road from Poperinghe to Ypres, the one good road running east and west. Yet in a critical moment an endless caravan of waggons and carts and panic-stricken men and women, loaded down with their burdens, shouted and jostled and moaned.

Transport of every sort was drawn up on the pathway, and some batteries of guns, awaiting orders. The moon had not yet risen, and the night was blacker than hell. The only way to get through was to blast a way, and this Jumbo did. Walking and riding—almost feeling the road—the cyclists cursed and damned a path through the craven *burghers* and the stolid gunners. And the refugees were whispering among themselves and shouting to the cyclists as they passed—

"The Boches are shelling Ypres as they never shelled it before."

Over the shouts and the curses, the rumble and the creaking and the moans, came the shattering crashes of enormous shells bursting, and a funny slight sound of roaring—the noise of flames.

They reached the gate of the *château* which was Advanced

Divisional Headquarters, and rode up the drive. The Staff Room had a quiet and scholarly air. The colonel, lean and black, took the Gaspipe and Jumbo over to an immense map which almost covered one wall of the room, and expounded the situation as if he were lecturing to a mixed audience on Ricardo's Theory of Rent.

All the information he had was that the Germans by employing gas had driven back the French from the Langemarck line. One of the cyclist patrols was to ride through Ypres to St Julien and report on the position there. The Canadians might have been compelled to bring back slightly and adjust their left brigade. The second patrol was to ride along the western bank of the Yperlee Canal to Boesinghe, find out from the French there exactly what had happened, cross the canal, and proceed back along the road that runs a mile or so to the north-east of the canal.

"I do not think," he concluded judicially, "that the vague reports that have reached us and the surmises we have been compelled to make point to the fact of an enemy force on or in the neighbourhood of the north bank of the canal."

The Gaspipe was to take the canal patrol, for he spoke some pidgin French. Outside the Staff Room, Smith, the A.D.C., met him.

"Have a drink, old man, before you go out?"

The Gaspipe refused. He was wondering what would happen if an enemy force was in the neighbourhood of the canal. . . .

He pushed off into the deserted outskirts of Ypres and turned to the left just after crossing the railway. There was a trifling lull in the shelling. He rode easily with eyes and ears well open. The moon was rising in a clear sky. Along the canal all was quiet. Some Canadian engineers had heard only that the French had been driven back. A mile on he came to a temporary bridge held by *Zouaves*. Trenches were being hastily dug. There was a certain feverish activity.

"We do not know what is going on," an officer replied; "but something terrible is happening on our left."

Ahead there seemed to be much noise of rifles and machine-guns and some shelling. The nervousness with which the Gaspipe had started left him. The affair was interesting.

Just south of Boesinghe the railway crosses the Yperlee Canal and the Dixmuide-Ypres road, which is the road that runs along the western bank of the canal. Fifty yards from the level-crossing is a ruined cottage. There the Gaspipe left four men and his sergeant, because the village was most undoubtedly being shelled. He walked into the village with the remaining man, and meeting a corporal, asked him the way to the French Headquarters. The corporal replied in a string of words, among which "marmite" and "*château*" predominated.

"Headquarters are in a *château*, and it is being shelled," murmured the Gaspipe wisely. "*En avant, mon vieux.*"

The corporal cheerily led the way through the main street of the village, and he laughed out loud when the nose and eyes of the Gaspipe began freely to smart and water. Then the Gaspipe noticed that the village was filled with a greenish mist. Whatever it was, it was damnably unpleasant. He felt for a handkerchief and found he had none. It was awkward to interview a French general when one's nose was running and there was no handkerchief to hand. This artificially inspired rheum was a bore.

They came to the lodge gate of the *château*, so, taking leave of the cheery corporal, the Gaspipe and his man walked steadily up the drive. Now, if you hear a shell coming, you can do one of two things—get down or stop up. To get down is always the wiser course, but to get down and then to hear the shell pass harmlessly over your head and burst quarter of a mile farther on is to lose one's self-respect and the respect of others.

To choose aright requires expert knowledge. On the other hand, if you know that with the very shell you hear the Hun is trying to slaughter *you*, don't think at all. Get down. The Gaspipe heard a shell coming and pressed himself flat to the ground. The Germans were endeavouring to hit the *château*, and the *château* was only fifty yards away.

The shell whistled and roared. The Gaspipe thought for a

flash absurdly that khaki is invisible in the dark. There was a terrific explosion—just by his right ear, it seemed. All sorts of soft things fell on to his back. He jumped up before the smoke had cleared away.

"All right, Bloomfield?"

"I think so, sir" very feebly "but I can't see."

The Gaspipe seized him and dragged him at a run to the side of the *château*, determined in his panic that he would not be between the *château* and the Hun when the next shell arrived: but the next shell, disdainful of mere human reason, burst beyond the *château*. "Marmite" and "*château*" an unpleasant combination.

He was ushered ceremoniously along dark corridors, a door was flung open, and he stood in an immense room full of tarnished finery. At a table on the right sat the general and his staff. To the left were the orderlies—behind some indefinite figures.

The general looked up and saw an immense, long, khaki figure, bespattered with mud and leaves, and wiping his nose continuously on the sleeve of his coat. Queer people, these British!

The Gaspipe advanced and made a ceremonious bow.

Bon soir, mon général—les compliments du général du cinquième division, le fameux cinquième division qui était à Mons (snuffle)—et il veut savoir que se fait—que passe—en bref, quelle est la situation ici.

The general, an upright white-haired old man, came forward, shook hands warmly, and began to explain. This is the drift of what he said, or rather what the Gaspipe understood him to say.

Give my most respectful compliments to your general. I have heard much of your famous division. The situation is altogether horrible! The Boches are uncivilised brutes. At about five o'clock this afternoon there was a cannonade along the line of the brigade which I have the happiness to command. It was nothing much. Then my brave men, ready for anything in reason, saw approaching them rolling greenish clouds. It was the atrocious gas. They are brave—they are brave, I say, but they could do nothing.

They were overwhelmed, crushed, massacred. The remnant retired, and the Boches pursued them. Ah, it was atrocious. We have fallen back about four kilometres, and now we are holding the line of the canal. The Germans are only two hundred metres on the other side of the canal here.
Of the French division on my right—between my brigade and the Canadians—I have heard nothing, know nothing. Their headquarters are at Elverdinghe, but they have not communicated with me.

The old man sat down again very sorrowfully. His brigade-major murmured something in his ear.

Ah, les contre-attaques! Yes, I have ordered counterattacks at Het Sas and Steenstraate, and we hope that the division on my right will attack the Germans at Pilkem, on their flank.

The Gaspipe made notes on his map, asked many questions concerning the tactical disposition of the French forces, and bowed himself out gracefully.

The shelling had ceased, but the village rattled and rang with rifle and mitrailleuse. Just before the railway-crossing there are no houses on the north side of the street. He hesitated—then took to the ditch, but the water was deep, and stank; so, pulling himself together, he took to the road again, and, running across the open spaces, came safely to the ruined cottage where he had left his men.

There he sat down, borrowed a handkerchief, blew his nose tremendously, and in a minute or so was able to see his notebook. In the meantime, he was cheered by a shell which skimmed the cottage and burst harmlessly in a field on the other side of the road. He wrote a brief report, and gave it to Bloomfield, who was off in a flash.

Obviously, it was impossible to cross the canal, because the Germans were on the farther side. He determined to ride back, and, crossing whatever bridges there might be, find out exactly where the line was.

They raced away to the first bridge. Leaving his men, he walked across. In five minutes, he returned with the desired information, and made a mental note: Germans four hundred metres from canal.

The ride to the next (Canadian) bridge was not without excitement. The Germans had either pushed forward or woken up during the last two hours. Bullets *zeep-pinged* overhead, and shrapnel intended for the road burst just beyond it. There was an empty feeling in the Gaspipe's stomach. Charitably, he put it down to hunger.

They again dismounted at the Canadians' bridge. 'From an officer on the east side the Gaspipe heard roughly how the line ran. At this point the Germans were beginning to use high explosive, so, pushing through some Canadian waggons, he turned off westwards, picked his way through some lanes, and arrived triumphantly at the *château*.

Although his nose was running and his eyes smarted—the first made him red and awkward: why hadn't he brought a handkerchief?—he determined to bathe in the academic atmosphere of the Staff Room.

"We have received your report," said the colonel; "please tell the general the details of the situation."

Imagine, then, the Gaspipe holding forth bravely—punctuating each sentence with a snuffle and a shamed wipe of sleeve across nose. On the way back he had put all the facts in fine order. A red-tabbed audience, a large map, and the academic atmosphere inspired him to produce what he himself felt was a nicely-rounded little lecture. . . .

The French left brigade was back on the canal. He doubted whether the canal could be held, for the nerves of the men were badly shaken, and there remained only three weak battalions. The French right division had disappeared, save for a battalion or two who were holding a position in such-and-such a square. The left flank of the Canadians was badly afloat. Indeed, there appeared to be a gap between the Canadians and the right of the French remnant. The Germans, however, did not seem to be pushing through. He suspected they had not looked for such success. Their position was in square so-and-so. . . .

He ended. Sundry questions were asked and answered, and then he was sent out again to keep a watch on the canal until the whole company had time to ride up and take over.

So, they started off back again, a little tired and stale. At the Canadian bridge there was more and more high explosive. They rode carefully northwards, cursing on the way some cyclists of another division who were careering madly along on the wrong side of the road. The German shrapnel was still bursting a hundred yards or so to the west of the road. Once more the Gaspipe felt that empty feeling in the stomach, and this time he put it down to fear. He was thinking too much of what would happen if the Germans registered accurately.

He had told the staff that he would make a cottage just opposite the French bridge his headquarters. Fifty yards from it *Zouaves* were holding a line between the road and the canal. The Germans seemed to be on the other bank, from the noise of the rifles and the fierce singing of their bullets across the road. He heard a little sad sob and then another. Two of the blue figures that had been standing fell to the ground and lay there.

He came to the cottage and, dismounting his men, began to lead them behind it. Suddenly the air was nothing but a sheet of white flame—an unbearable, monstrous crash, as if the world were falling to bits. Something pressed down upon him hard, and then his right leg gave way queerly. He hung on to his bicycle, trembling and stooping. He put his leg to the ground. It was all right, he could walk. Gently he murmured—

"By God, that was near. It does shake one up!"

His bicycle fell from his hand as he turned round and shouted, "All right, Ray?"

There was no answer—only a low groaning and a wee scream. In the sallow light lay a heap of shattered bicycles and men, all muddled confusedly together. He limped into the middle of them.

"Ray, old man, aren't you all right? What's happened, Ray?"

There was no answer—only a groan and a wild loud cry—"My leg! My leg!"

Then a man slowly raised himself and stood up, shaking all over and holding his right hand with his left. The blood fell in great drops.

"Here I am, sir—they've got us this time. Oh, my hand!"

The correct thing under the circumstances, thought the Gaspipe grimly, is to get these men under cover before another beggar comes along. The road is distinctly unhealthy from (*a*) shells, (*b*) bullets.

They searched among the heaps and found a man who had been hit in the head. Very roughly they made him understand what he was to do. Then together, painfully and slowly, they carried the men, one by one, behind the farm and propped them up against the wall. The last time they went out a cow mooed. Both of them started violently—the Gaspipe laughed. He felt almost genial.

"Ray, old sport, our nerves are not what they were."

Leaving Ray and a Frenchman he had found in charge of the men, he picked up his bicycle and started for the Canadians to find a doctor. He had ridden a little way, when there was a crash behind him. Nearly falling from his bicycle, he pedalled furiously in panic fear to the Canadian bridge. There he waited until a doctor was discovered. After giving the doctor full directions, he turned off again past the Canadian waggons. A parting shell burst in a field beside him.

It was all so melodramatic. How could he report to the division without being melodramatic? But the road was heavy and crowded, and his leg was weak. Near the *château* he looked towards Ypres. The Great Tower was silhouetted against vast tongues of crude flame. The city was burning fiercely—as if some wrathful god had walked into it and lit monstrous bonfires. There was a rumbling and a clattering, and great distant thuds.

He walked into the Staff Room and leant against a chair, feeling sick. How absurd it would be to vomit in that academic atmosphere! The colonel was dictating a long message. It seemed an age before he looked up.

"Yes?"

"I am sorry to report, sir, that my patrol has been knocked out—shrapnel. I thought I had better come back, sir, to report."

Then Baylor came in and took him into the pantry to have a glass of wine. He told his story, and finished with the great news.

"Baylor, I've got a cushy wound!"

They shook hands, and Baylor congratulated him jealously. The wound was displayed, a neat little red hole, and dressed. Everybody congratulated him.

"We'll send you along in the sidecar to the nearest dressing-station," said Baylor, "and they'll hoike it out for you. Come along!"

8. Cold Chicken and Champagne

The Gaspipe Officer squeezed himself into the sidecar and waited fearfully for thrills: Tommy's eye judged in quarter inches, particularly when gunners with restive horses were about. They dashed fiercely down the drive, stopped abruptly for a divisional car, and swung off into the spate of traffic on the road from Ypres to Poperinghe. By this time, it was flowing with some slight attempt at reasoned order.

The monster waggons and high-loaded carts of the now resigned refugees were stranded hopelessly in the mud at the side. The military had usurped the firm centre. Guns and multitudinous ammunition limbers were moving up—wearily, like people waiting their turn at the door of a theatre. Motor ambulances and empty waggons were hurrying west from the poor old stricken city. The flare of the great burning in Ypres cast queer little shadows.

Through it all Tommy steered a wizard course, charming to the trained eye of his cargo. There was a noise of great swearing—Bill and the rest of the company.

"Hi, Bill! Patrol's knocked out. Got a scrap in my leg. Going to have it hooked out. Be with you in the morning. No, just a cushy wound. So long! Good luck!"

They wriggled in and out past the cyclists, who were loudly worming their way through the crush, rattled into Vlamertinghe, and swung left on to the quietude of the Ouderdom road. "Granny" and her enormous train still lay inert close up to the friendly wall of an *estaminet*. Her slaves, the gunners, stared towards Ypres. . . .

Stopping outside the camp, Tommy ran in to fetch Brown and the Gaspipe's kit. A cable cart crawled hesitatingly along.

"Would you mind moving that sidecar?"

"Sorry, I can't; (proudly) been hit in the leg."

Profuse apologies and interesting inquiries. A couple of men pushed the sidecar very carefully out of the way. The hero was reminded of a time when he had pushed his grandmother down a steep place with a little violence.

Tommy returned, and they jolted over the painful *pavé* to the advanced section of a Field Ambulance. The doctor was hoarse, and talked mechanically, as men do when they are inhumanly weary. The little room stank of iodine and blood and some cast- or cut-off clothes that lay piled in a corner. Iodine was slopped into the wound and a careful injection made. Then the Gaspipe became heroic.

"I think I'll try and walk back to camp."

"All right," said the doctor carelessly.

The first ten paces were a triumph, the second a bore, and the third a torture. He hobbled back on the arm of the faithful Brown.

"Sorry to trouble you again, doctor; I'm afraid you must put me up."

"Thought so," replied the doctor dryly, and offered his own bed. The Gaspipe refused, and settled down finally on a stretcher. He slept a trifle, but for the most part spent the night in cursing his leg.

At the welcome dawn he was lifted into an ambulance, find-ing there Springett, one of his patrol, who had been hit on the head—not too seriously. This lad had walked a couple of miles on the unhealthiest of roads to obtain help and stretchers, when the doctor that the Gaspipe thought he had secured did not come, obtained them, and made a couple of journeys, carrying his comrades into safety. All this the Gaspipe heard afterwards from Bill.

They came to Reninghelst, where the Gaspipe was labelled

and given breakfast, then on slowly to Poperinghe, the most wearisome of journeys. He was put on a little bed in an ante-room that formed part of a corridor. There was a door into it and a door out of it. Both were always banging, banging. A nurse smiled and asked if his wound were dressed. At last an orderly came and offered him food—cold chicken and champagne! He blessed the giver.

One door led down into a sunken hall crammed full of wounded officers. Most of them were waiting cheerfully for the hospital train, and a fair number left late in the morning, but oases kept coming in. An ambulance would arrive and be unloaded. This you knew by the intermittent shriek of pain, and the hectic complaints of the nerve-shattered wounded that reverberated horribly along the corridors.

There would be a shriek and a long crooning wail—then little childish moans and chatter.

"Oh, do take care. It does hurt so. Move slowly. It burns like anything. Oh, it does hurt. G—d d—n you, man, be careful, be careful! Oh, it does hurt so."

The long crooning wail would begin again.

Some men were brought in, yellow and gasping. The noises they made shivered in your spine. These were the first victims of the gas. . . . The day passed with diabolical slowness. The staff, ever kind, listening reasonably to the most unreasonable of complaints, kept telling how overcrowded they were and how the hospital trains were being delayed by the supply trains with ammunition.

The narrow ante-room begun to fill with "sitting-up cases." There was the subaltern who had blown up Hill 60, and a bunch of young Canadians who talked of affrays in western saloons, camping in far forests, and the price of land.

One lad stumbled in and sat down in a heap. His mouth kept twitching and his eyes were never still. They asked him where he had been hit.

"Not wounded. One shell just to right and one shell just to left. Picked myself up. Nerve gone."

At every sound he shuddered. When the door banged, he started as if someone had struck him and cringed fearfully. He would forget himself for a moment and talk feverishly of gasconading days and purple nights in Canadian saloons. The door banged, and again he would cringe and moan and mutter about his nerves.

When it grew dark food was brought—cold chicken and champagne. They ate enormous meals; most of them had been without food for many hours.

There was talk of a hospital train at 8, and then at 10, but the summons never came. Restlessly they sat and could speak of nothing except the train. For the ante-room was so crowded that only a few could sit down. The rest leant against the wall or squatted on the floor. As it grew later, they tried to settle themselves to sleep. The Gaspipe, hobbling out into the corridor, found a stretcher and Brown made him up some sort of bed. He dozed fitfully, wakened by the noise of motor ambulances loading and unloading, the groans and cries of the wounded, and a certain unpleasantness in a nether limb.

About four in the morning he was wakened finally by a gruff voice—"Up with you! Get a move on! The ambulances are going."

Another long wait on the chilly steps and they were sitting comfortably in an ambulance. The convoy fled away along the Steenvoorde road, past dark columns of slow waggons, past interminable columns of French and English guns—away through Hazebrouck.

They reached St Omer in the grey of the morning and drew up at a forbidding-looking infirmary. They hobbled or were carried up innumerable steps and deposited in a cheerful ward, where they were given hot tea and put to bed. It was extraordinarily comfortable, and the Gaspipe, for one, never again wanted to move. There was no noise of guns and no endless rattling of transport over cobbles. Everybody was kind and quiet. Besides, being wounded, he had become a personage to be tended and cared for, a man whom all delighted to honour. . . .

In a couple of hours, it was announced that the lighter cases were to go straight to Boulogne. So, the Gaspipe dressed and, after telling the true story of the night of the 22nd to "Eyewitness," was bundled downstairs into a motor ambulance and thence into a hospital train.

They were cherished mightily in that train by a dear nurse who had the Bulgarian medal, and a young doctor who was pathetically eager to supply all wants. The lunch was foretold but the prophecy was false. The cold chicken came, just as good as it had ever been, and—beer.

The Gaspipe travelled down with a young French Canadian and an oldish subaltern. Beyond Boulogne—the sun was setting—the subaltern exclaimed at the play of light on a pink-and-yellow cutting. It was A——, the artist.

So, they came to Etaples. The Gaspipe was informed that he was going to the Hospital of the Duchess. He was lifted into a car with more tenderness than he required, and together with Mirfield, who had been shot through the arm, was whirled along straight, dimly-lit avenues of dark trees to the glowing front of a Casino.

9. The Hospital of the Duchess

When the Gaspipe had been told that he was being sent to the Hospital of the Duchess, he did not know whether to laugh or cry. Behind the line rumours had trickled through of perfectly charming but perilously inefficient nurses, whose milk-white hands would nervously fumble with the wound, whose chatter was so delicious that it kept you awake, who sat on your bed just where it would hurt you, and then apologise so sweetly that you forgot the throb; who sometimes, when you were very good and kept yourself clean, kissed you goodnight.

To an 'ero slightly wounded these were pleasant anticipations: yet behind them lurked the thought that a cushy and altogether gentlemanly wound can become a right royal disablement under ignorant care.

He had also heard of other hospitals, very different. In these, elderly and harsh featured spinsters with large red hands tyrannised with a horrible efficiency. You were regarded as a Case—and only those most painfully and interestingly disfigured were treated with any consideration. You would see a prophetic gleam in the nurse's eye. She would dose you and starve you until you were ready for the Operation, the high-water mark of hospital existence. Then, most indecently unarrayed, you would be stretched on a cold, white and shiny table, and, in the presence of a group of ghoulish spectators, be cut scientifically. Afterwards you were violently sick. . . .

During the first few moments the Hospital of the Duchess seemed surely of the former type. He was carried into an immense white entrance-hall where a few cheerful wounded sat critical of the incomers, and nurses, delightfully attired, appeared and disappeared through mysterious doors.

One of them watched the new arrivals with such a kind and melancholy-sympathetic countenance that the Gaspipe, whose leg had ceased to throb, was compelled through very pride to cringe momentarily as though in pain. With enormous care he was lifted upstairs and into a cosy little ward of ten or twelve beds. It seemed nothing but whiteness and light and cheerfulness. Two nurses approached him, hiding their sorrow at his condition under a brave smile. He was put to bed, and in a little there came a simple well-cooked dinner on trays.

The ward was more than luxurious—it was comfortable. Everything was neat and well-ordered. There were cigarettes and flowers by each bedside, and a little library at the end of the room.

He was puzzled. The Hospital of the Duchess was a discreet combination of the rumoured types, both decorative and efficient. And the men downstairs called it "more than an 'ome from 'ome." Was this hospital, then, supreme, of a perfect type equalled by none other? They liked to think so. Or perhaps it is only of the few extremer hospitals that they had heard. Most of them may be like the Hospital of the Duchess. . . .

About half past seven the curtains would be drawn, and the night sister disappear into a hidden place from which she would bring tea and biscuits with the help of the orderly. Afterwards there was washing and shaving and dressing. No one who has not been inside a hospital can imagine how interesting these everyday processes can become. So many questions arise.

If a man is wounded in the knee and cannot bend his leg without pain, should he or should he not wash his feet? For it was a point of honour to leave as little washing as possible to sister and orderly. Does sister want to rub and powder my back this morning? How much dressing can a man with one arm do for himself? Will sister dress me today, or will she leave it to the orderly?

Everybody shaved himself who could. The official shaver was an old sick-berth attendant, and had been used to rougher skins. He swore that he could shave you if you were standing on your head, and boasted of the fact that he was the only orderly in hospital who could shave men in bed. He lied in his mouth. True, he could tie a strop to your bedpost and make much play with the razor. He could lather you well into the eyes and mouth, and then wonder why you were not interested in his reminiscences. But shave? No! All the great barbers of old times and today, the barbers of Florence, and Pass and Truefitt, would cry out against the slander. Rather did he take a length of dull metal that dragged out the hairs reluctantly one by one. It was a tug of war in which the hair, bloody and bowed, but still retaining the greater portion of its old Adam, stood victorious; for the would-be razor showed its acerbity only on the softer spots, where it would rage and bite deep into the quivering flesh. I have heard it said by a patient that he would rather undergo another operation. . . .

Then came a pleasant breakfast and a pipe. It should have been a joyous meal. Everybody was clean and shaved and attired for the day. The night had ended for those who could not sleep. But after breakfast came dressings and the putting of shattered and shrinking limbs into baths, and other things unpleasant that only the cheerfulness of the old surgeon made tolerable.

So, with talk and the reading of books and writing of letters till lunch-time. In the afternoon the stronger brethren were allowed out to walk in the pine-woods, saunter along the beach, take tea with their friends, or play mild badminton with the sisters. The beds of the others would on sunny days be taken out on the balcony, a doubtful pleasure.

The curative properties of the sun's rays are probably immense, but the wilful wind would find its way with a worm-like persistence into the bed's *arcana*, blow over your tobacco, and make the reading of a newspaper a herculean struggle. When the beds were taken in, it was time for tea.

Everybody rejoiced when Mrs Witherington, or Jackson's

sister, visited her brother at tea-time. It was not merely that she brought her brother chocolates and sweets and cakes, which were inevitably passed round. She smiled so nicely, and radiated such pleasant goodwill, that for a time they all forgot their aches and pains.

So, the day passed till dinner. Some, scarcely troubled by their hurts, just basked in the quietude and cleanliness and comfort. For others the day consisted of long periods of pain between the short agonies of having their wounds dressed. . . .

Hambledon was a study in yellow and mauve, for he had jaundice and mauve silk pyjamas. When he was not scratching, he flirted outrageously or chaffed the night sister. One morning the doctor told him he was well enough to be moved. From then on, he lived in a giggling state of almost restless excitement—till the hour came.

Jackson was their oldest inhabitant. He had lost an arm. Young and dark, he was overflowing with good-humoured wit, and scintillated with anecdote and allusion. His cross-chat to the Sister when she dressed him was a joy. The ward was dull without Jackson.

Then there was Healy, the voluble journalist, recovered from bronchitis, and Carrier, the mountaineering doctor, who had cut his toes while showing some men how to fell a tree. When he was not telling them tales of his patients and his partner, he would spend his time in discussing with the authorities, over reams of paper, whether he was accidentally wounded or not, and which army form they should have issued. Old B—— lay patient and always cheerful, though his thigh was riddled with tubing; and Mirfield, the cricketer, after a hard struggle, kept his arm. They were a very pleasant company. . . .

Doctors should be sure of their own minds. The Gaspipe was to be operated on in the afternoon. Accordingly, he was dosed and starved, and cheered by the others with full details of operations they had known. The result of it all was a particularly large tea, as the surgeon forgot, or somebody who was urgently dying had to be ushered out of the world with scientific exactitude.

This irregular feeding was repeated on the following day. Breakfast was attenuated with a view to ether, and a dose given. A local anaesthetic was finally decided upon, and lunch correspondingly increased. At the end the Gaspipe could not for his very life have told you whether he was empty or full.

They carried him away to a little white room, and laid him on a table that was much too short. Then they garbed themselves until they looked like members of one of those secret societies that nourish so rankly in Cinemaland. The theatre-sisters, who were perfectly charming, busied themselves, the anaesthetist was engaged in some trial squirts, the surgeon, a curious blend of a monk and Mr Carpenter in our childhood's *Happy Families*, selected an instrument or two, and the duchess stood by with cigarette and sympathy.

The supposed merit of novocaine is that you know but do not feel what is going on. To appreciate this, it is necessary to be a man of great faith. Novocaine is a local anaesthetic, extremely local—so local in fact that it is difficult indeed to find the *locus* or place which it affects.

A certain general said that man was put into this world to hunt. The surgeon agreed heartily with the general. A good half-hour was spent in hunting for the required scrap, in intervals for more anaesthetic refreshment, in warding off cigarette ash from things that mattered, and in acquiring a reputation for conversational facility under the most painful circumstances.

At last the patient felt a harsh grating, and his murmured request for a trifle more anaesthetic was drowned in the triumph of the surgeon. A sharp cut, another, a particularly lusty twinge, and the tiny scrap of metal was brought out and presented to its owner. Everything was stitched up and cleared up. The Gaspipe returned to the congratulations of the ward.

During the night he understood the need for a night sister, hot milk, and aspirin. . . .

Since first he had realised the fact that he was wounded, he had wondered if there were any possibility of getting home. It was the beginning of May, and the leave of last December had already vanished like a dream. The authorities were chilling. He would be kept in hospital for the little time that was necessary for the leg to heal. Afterwards there would be light duty in Boulogne. But the doctor consented to aid him in trying his fate. A chit was prepared, and the hour and place discovered at which the Medical Board sat.

He dressed carefully, and took into the ambulance with him a small pair of crutches. He was whirled away along the dustiest roads through Etaples to Boulogne.

At the side of a ramshackle school there is a small wooden hut raised slightly from the ground. Outside, along the wall of the school, are some benches on the gravel. Many men sit on these benches and wait their turn hopefully. Some in their restlessness draw pictures in the gravel with their sticks. Others throw stones aimlessly on the roof of a yard. The name is called. The man enters. Brusquely he is questioned, cross-questioned, and examined. No verdict is given, though sometimes a hint is dropped. A day or two later the judgment is announced—a fortnight's sick-leave or light duty at the docks.

It was a long time before the Gaspipe's turn came. Then, his length hunched between the pigmy crutches, he valiantly assailed the steps. Twice he failed, and the third time he succeeded. This curiously impressed the board, and his frank assertion that he was perfectly well, so obviously belied by his infirmities, told in his favour. The board let drop a hint, and he stumped out joyously with more skill than discretion.

They lunched moderately well, and after some shopping drove down to the depot for some petrol. Here gather the motor-ambulance drivers, elderly men mostly, retired merchants and the like, only too glad to be able to make themselves useful. Few men of military age drive these motor ambulances, the Gaspipe was told. Those who are of age and have no excuse of unfitness are gently reminded, it was added, that their proper place is elsewhere. . . .

When they returned to the Hospital of the Duchess the dropped hint was analysed, discussed, and valued. Expert opinion favoured short leave of a fortnight. The word came late that night. The pigmy crutches had achieved their end. Next morning everything was hastily packed, and together with a slightly wounded intelligence officer the Gaspipe was driven down to the harbour.

10. Wounded 'Ero

In the first December of the war those on leave experienced fully the quiet pleasure of being honoured. Just as when a murder is committed, everybody who can claims some acquaintance with the characters of the crime the daughter of the murderer always makes a good marriage—so it was the delight of the Briton to cherish the man on leave. The muddied greatcoat had only to enter a car on the Tube and half the men would offer their seats. The women would nudge their husbands, and these, nervously daring, would sidle up and murmur in a deprecating voice: "You have been in France?"

Of course, nothing important resulted from this touching consideration. Only a few kindly and thoughtful men and women have tried to make leave worth its while. If you meet a gaunt, filthy, and joyous figure, you smile at him, naturally, and granted you are a gentleman of words, turn a neatly-rounded sentence on our brave defenders. You have never thought of organising a clearing house, of piloting your brave defenders safely home. And certainly you send your brave defenders back filled with the melancholy forebodings that are current among the best informed civilians. . . .

Still a wounded 'ero, particularly a wounded officer, has a tremendous time of it. When the boat reached Folkestone, special constables swept on board, throwing everybody aside to make room for the poor fellow with crutches. On landing, the Gas-pipe was fiercely attacked with offers of Bovril and cigarettes. He was despairing ever of reaching the train, when suddenly the mob evaporated. Afterwards he learnt the rumour had gone round that a certain queen was travelling *incognito* by the same boat. He seated himself in a Pullman and graciously accepted lunch from a sympathetic manufacturer. London and a long ride in a taxi through black streets . . . that is a far cry from Boesinghe to Burford—from those pitted, ochreous fields and noisy roads and tumbled, broken houses, and nights alive with fighting. The Gaspipe was assured that the war had hit the fourth valley of the Windrush hard.

Many had enlisted, and you never knew how late the local trains might be. There was no one in Northleigh or Witney or Burford or Widford who had not some friend or relative at the Front. Burford was full of tales. Timmins's Trouble, who before the war was ever playing truant and raiding orchards, had run away to Oxford and 'listed. Annie's young man had been blown out of his trench.

The Blue Goat no longer rang on Sunday afternoon with the laughter and jests of the young gentlemen from Oxford. Mary no longer blushed at the compliments she had received for the cakes of her own making. And those lads and girls who had brought to life again those old dances and songs, which the village folk learnt so quickly that they seemed always to have known them, no longer came and danced and rioted and made merry with the Blue Goat's fine old ale.

The war had hit Burford hard!

Yet the Gaspipe, back again in the coffee-room of the Blue Goat with the proud gramophone, the soberly shining pewter, the hideous chairs, and Mary lightly telling stories of the village, could scarcely remember anything save that day, when, hearing laughter in the courtyard, he had jumped from his bed to the window, and jeered at Alec for a too early walk; of the stroll after tea across the meadows to the old mass-chapel of St Oswald's-in-the-Fields, and home in the dusk along the Happy Valley, and how the spire of Burford Church sticks up absurdly from behind the shoulder of a hill; of the talk by the light of the fire, and how they wrote a little note to her mother, who had gone to bed, asking if Mary might stop up a trifle longer and charm away the thought of "Schools" from their aching heads; of the sharp tramp over the hill to Shipton-under-Wychwood.

In the Happy Valley there was no noise of the transport interminably rattling over cobbles. . . .

And Oxford, filled again with subalterns and gunners, Somerville become a hospital, and Oriel become Somerville—who will be left to carry on the traditions of wise folly and urgent, strenuous living? Will those who come after understand the thrilling pleasure in hiring the Masonic Hall for positively the first debate between Somerville and a college? They will never stroll down to the Paviers' and play shove-ha'penny with the Ancient Order of Buffaloes, debate on the two main methods of wearing pyjamas, see how the walls of Holywell become yellow and pink in the arc-light, shout their curious war-cry under Trinity windows, explore Venice and the goods-yard, suspect their political opponents of illegal breakfasts, or choose with a careful ignorance their favourite Burgundy. No, they will be a military race and despatch essays to their tutors, with covering note:—

Herewith required essay on *Lancastrian Experiment* (University Form No. 101. Undergraduate Co-operative Series). For your information and early return, please. Acknowledge.

Oxford is full now of shrouded remembrances, very present vulgarities and fears. . . .

There is one strong link to old time. The appearance of the wounded 'ero, passing discreetly and affectionately through, brought forth courteous reminders from sundry interested merchants. One night in Flanders we talked together and pictured these solid *burghers* carefully putting on their spectacles, running fat fingers down the casualty lists, and reading the names in terms of indebtedness. Yet surely, they must forgive us for our past omissions; their sons, too, are at the war.

We are doing our best to help, for Oxford is a broken city. The colleges are limping along, the weaker with the help of the stronger. But the landladies who used to batten on us have little custom. The dining places are silent and dismal. The shops charge "war" instead of "term" prices. Nobody now hires a horse. Nobody's motorcycle requires continuous repairs. The theatre is turned over to cheap varieties, and the streets that used to be gay are haggard—except for Timmins's Trouble and his fellows. . . .

So, the Gaspipe, leaving Oxford and its kindly dons and sharp-eyed tradesmen, came to a certain suburb. All the manhood of it had gone to the war, but little had changed. The mothers did not arrive home so soon after church, for their sons' deeds had to be explained and compared. Tennis parties became feminine and croquet was re-learnt for the benefit of the wounded 'eroes. Yet all the small important policies and politics, alliances and enmities, came out again in the new war-work. The Supply Depot had to be carefully organised on a social basis, and discipline was enforced and regretted as discipline always is.

The stringent class distinctions of the suburbs became loosened. Had not John, the butcher's son, got his commission? Suspected spies were treated with whispering coldness, and much alacrity was shown in the dimming of neighbours' lights. Everybody strongly represented to everybody else what everybody else's particular war-work should be. If someone came and spoke to you, the someone was interfering unwarrantably with your personal liberty. If you tactfully spoke to your neighbour, you were performing an unpleasant but patriotic duty.

The conventions, too, were disregarded. Girls travelled up to London to their war-work by themselves—and the girl postwoman, who had never had a better time in her life, received much sympathy.

Then there was the burning question of military age and fitness. In such a friendly family suburb no one might decide for himself. Other people's chauffeurs were eyed darkly, and the age of one's own gardener was kept in misty doubt. Suspicion fell upon wounded officers who required too long a convalescence, and merely to drive a motor ambulance was more criminal than to remain at home and still flutter on the Stock Exchange. The

Gaspipe had never before realised what the driving power of a community, bound together in mutual rivalry and composed mainly of women, can finally achieve. . . .

Again, there were optimists and pessimists and strategists. One dear old lady believed that the war could be ended if only the *Kaiser* could be captured. She could not understand why we did not concentrate on this all-important end. Another ran round her garden every morning before breakfast, so that if the Huns came, she might run and hide herself in the jungle. A third practised vigorously with a revolver, so that she might shoot at least one German, even if in punishment the whole suburb were destroyed.

The more dolorous papers were assiduously read, and in our suburb, it is firmly believed that the Germans can detach a million from one front, throw it against another, wipe up the Serbians, land in Syria, and return before the absence has been noticed. Everything English is good, but silly: everything German is wicked, but wise. With a charitable toleration it has been decided that all Germans must be exterminated like rats, though at the same time we must, of course, retain our fair fame and fight only as gentlemen should.

The suburb is like a small, busy, contentious town of old Greece. The Gaspipe wondered idly what would happen if the suburb and Hulluch were suddenly to change places. . . .

So, to London which swallowed up the war or thought of it. Tottenham Court Road was still that odd mixture of gross sensation and business. Cross & Blackwell's had the same ineffable odour. The bookshops off and on the Charing Cross Road had not changed. Leicester Square was still an oasis for a pipe-smoker in a desert of convention. The top of Bloomsbury Square had not altered since that famous murder had been attempted for the delectation of a respectable old man. At dusk the river, the sky, and the chimneys of the Station were as blue as they had ever been from Cheyne Walk.

And a decadent review, full of the old audacities and clevernesses, came out to welcome us home. . . .

The reader must forgive this slight chapter. It is written for the pleasure of remembrance in a tiny workman's cottage—the country is the dirtiest in the world, and there is a distant rumbling of transport, and of guns, and humming of aeroplanes. He will soon return to France.

1. The New Company

It is a starlit night with no moon, dark on the road and very still. Through the window drifts the heavy odour of the horses and the broken sound of their champing and uneasy movement. There is a certain liveliness tonight—the little thumps of the field-guns, the deeper interrupting boom of the big guns, the deliberate tapping of the machine guns, and, if you listen, you can hear the soft crackle of the rifles. Half a mile away a solitary waggon is rattling and creaking over the *pavé* of the great high-road. The engines whistle at the distant station.

From the factory drones a monotonous slow hum. In the next cottage a woman is weeping quietly in the gloom of her room and listening: the news came suddenly while she was scrubbing the floor for Sunday. It is midnight, and the company should be sleeping peacefully after a hard day. But an officer, hearing the discontented thunder and idle chatter and rumble of the guns and the rifles, is wondering how the old Fifth is faring many miles away.

By chance a despatch-rider, warned for the next "priority," may read this. Let him know there is one who would give much to be sent once more to find the divisional train, or even take some maps to the 14th. Why, these divisional trains in the new divisions don't realise that it is possible for them to be clean lost with motorcyclists sweeping the country for them! In those days the train was merely the train, the efficient, vagrant, humble servant of the fighting man.—And is old Ginger cooking still for the Headquarters' Section?

Next motorcyclist, please! The 15th are in this farm just off the main road where this wood begins. No, I can't lend you a map. This is the only map we have. Hurry up, you're all out now except old Grimers. . . .

Those who spent last winter and spring in Flanders have never seen the famous "emergency blue," know nothing of the travail that produced a battalion from a mob, had not even met the horrid blast of patriotic songs. The New Armies were to them what the latest favourites of Cinemaland are to the leaveless now, interesting novelties that make those returning feel dowdy. Still, these New Armies could come to the 'osses without a cackle. Somebody even ventured that it would be a fine job to see a battalion grow and help it through its pains. There was much speculation, and accounts were eagerly read.

Like many another junior sub., the Gaspipe, after a delicious convalescence and soft lazy weeks, when to all seeming everybody official had forgotten him, found that he was parted finally from the "the Div." and posted to the Irish Cyclists.

He had served "the Div." in that sweltering march to Bavai and to Dour: in the sullen retreat to Reumont: on that tragical day and ghastly night of Le Cateau: through the weary days and wearier nights of the Retreat: over the Marne, when, tired but triumphant, it had stumbled after the enemy: during the hard days of the Aisne and the hardest days of all by La Bassée and Ypres: through the patient winter of the trenches, the slaughter of Hill 60 and the excitements of Boesinghe.

From the hot morning when Bill and his cyclists had tasted blood north of the Mons Canal the division had been in the line or marching or travelling. And the Signal Company, the cyclists, his platoon—he was to leave all these and go to a "new" division. . . .

The Gaspipe departed for his first command, and in course of time the train came to a little Irish town. A car brought him to D.H.Q. The staff was interviewed, and finally he was set down at a gate. He waded through mud as sticky as any in Flanders, to tents round and in which some men were resting. A fat sergeant was tending a supercilious goat. His work gave an air of energy to an otherwise unconvincing scene. These were the Irish Cyclists. It was necessary to stalk in. . . .

In the afternoon the company was paid, and dismay entered the heart of the Gaspipe, who recalled a line of men carefully cleaned and brushed, briskly saluting. And that night he slept in a tent for the first time.

Early next morning they moved into the roomy barracks of the Irish town.

This "new Div." was formed when the "old Div." was fighting at La Bassée. First, there would be a handful of officers, some in mufti, and a few N.C.O.'s. They would drill each other, and be grateful for the opportunity, until the men arrived. From battalions still in embryo men were demanded to form a Cyclist Company. The wise selected carefully and the foolish sent their worst. These bunches of men were trained separately for a while, then brought together and the company formed.

Think, then, of this company a strange and ignorant but hotly enthusiastic crowd slowly becoming disciplined, men and officers learning for themselves—picking up cyclist work from an obsolete textbook and the fierce advice of the staff, with scarce a cycle or rifle among them. They struggled hard in the face of enormous difficulties and the vilest weather, until something began to emerge. It was rough and cheerful, keen and blundering, but a company.

Those must have been great days, at Mallow, Ballyvonare, and Ballyhooly, when everybody was experimenting, discussing, and most thoroughly enjoying life. Sometimes they grew disconsolate in the mud. Sometimes the division seemed to be left too much by itself to muddle along. Things happened very slowly, but some time they must go out.

We who thought ourselves old campaigners, but were young enough to be cynical, had laughed at the burning desire that flared through the letters from those in the New Armies at home. Surely, they couldn't be as eager as all that to experience the discomfort and the danger! There must be a bit of pose in it. When we came home, we knew the truth. It was a muddled emotion, compounded variously of patriotism, impatience with routine, and a craving for excitement—but it made these new divisions. "When we go out"—it was an ultimate event which they could scarcely picture. Certainly, they could not look beyond it. They used to debate furiously and uselessly about it just as we out here debate about the end of the war.

It became almost an academic problem. And when one circumstance after another pointed to the nearness of the day—when musketry was finished and all equipment was issued when we were *ready*, the excitement was tense and breathless. . . . There is no romance surely like the raising of vast armies. Out of lawless crowds of sturdy individuals respecting themselves too much, are fashioned splendid instruments that the careful general can confidently use. It is a hideous and magnificent pastime.

At Fermoy the company was "breeched." The gigantic barrack square and all the paraphernalia of a measured and orderly barrack life gave pride and discipline. There were opportunities, too, that mud and a cramped existence in tents had never provided. And the rain was not so persistent—while the new C.O. realised that military life was extraordinarily complicated. He fell suddenly into a new and rigidly unsympathetic world of Army Forms and States and Returns and Traditions and Rules.

Set in this world, entirely unfamiliar, he stood between his three hundred Irishmen and a swarm of institutions—offices and personages who fed, supplied, paid, and inspected his men. Then in ruling these Irishmen he must be a cautious and understanding despot. Nine months had taught him a few of the vices and virtues of the English mercenary, but these Irishmen, waking up dimly to a consciousness of the fact that they were soldiers, were just about as different from the Englishmen as they could be. That was where Cicero came in.

Cicero had been one of the company's midwives and was now second in command. He knew something about Irishmen and something about army forms, so the Gaspipe, throwing himself on Cicero's knowledge of the men, endeavoured to learn, in an inconspicuous way, something about army forms.

"Now, Cicero, how would you reply to this? Of course, each division has its own rules, and you in the New Army work things not quite in our way"—thus assuming the superiority of the Regular, but in reality making a pathetic search for information. So, the Gaspipe, too, learned, as is the New Army method, by teaching and his mistakes. He learned, like those famous Highlanders in K(l), to play the Round Game, laugh at the Practical Joke department, make love to the Fairy Godmother, and treat inspections in a proper perspective.

He found out that no self-respecting medical officer makes an inspection without finding something wrong. If one day the doctor objects to bread in quarters, they pass the word along for the bread to be well hidden in the remaining stairs. He discovered that the papers, by their great campaign against waste, had made life miserable for all commanding officers. Inspectors were ever coming round. They would poke their noses into refuse-tub and cook-house, then, turning sharply to him, fiercely demand—

"And what do you do with your surplus dripping?"

To which the best answer was that you had a bread-pudding on Monday to finish up the surplus bread—an idea which intrigued the inspectors greatly.

But training went forward. The company began to find itself. The unfit were weeded out and packed off to an infantry battalion, where presumably they were weeded out again. Excellent recruits came in. The men began to take a pride in what they did. How the men of No. 3 walked on air when the general praised their guard and awarded them the prize for competition drill! They began with one accord to despise the infantry, and that was the most hopeful sign.

Peter, who had sailed as engineer all over the globe in liners, tramps, and every kind of ship, and had driven hard *coolie* crews and *lascars* and stout white men, would stand in the middle of the barrack square, make his platoon ride round it for hours, and by dogged swearing and an infinite care for detail, train them until each man rode in his allotted place as if mesmerised. Did the wretched lag when he should have sprinted, or sprint when he should have lagged? An awful rumbling would come from the middle of the square, followed trippingly by a wild blast of Spanish invective.

If some evening in Flanders you see a platoon of cyclists riding with perfect interval along a straight and cobbled road, caring nothing for mud or lorry, then know that this is Peter's platoon; for although Peter has left us to organise a factory as the workers are girls he is sorely handicapped his gruff voice is still humbly and affectionately remembered:

"*Madre Dios!* Call that a line!—It's more like a dog's hind leg!"

Then there was Fitz, who had rushed home from Chile. Fitz would give his last pair of breeches to one of his men. He was in charge, too, of the Signallers, and the Gaspipe began to know that preparatory smile—

"Don't you think, sir, we might buy two signal-lamps out of the C.O.'s fund?"

If Fitz had had his way, all his men would have crossed to fight the Hun clothed in the purplest of purple and the finest of fine linen and his signallers would have marched proudly between twenty or thirty waggons containing their equipment.

George, Schnapps, Bill from the Far East, and the irrepressible Child—they all worked their hardest to bring nearer that day when the dreaded inspector, whoever he might be, would give the certificate of fitness.

And behind it all was a deeper feeling. These were the cyclists of the Irish Division. The Irish brigade was billeted in the town. Only those who know Ireland and Irishmen can know what that meant. . . .

A rumour trickled through that the division was going to England to complete its training. That was half the battle. In Ireland they felt they were forgotten and neglected, but if they went to England the day must be coming near. All available sources were searched to discover how long divisions remained at Aldershot or Salisbury before they embarked. Surely they could not be left to spend another Christmas. . . .

The order was given, and the Child, to his huge delight, was left in charge to clean up. At the harbour they marched along a narrow lane between two surging crowds, triumphant but embarrassed.

"Eh, misther, and will the Dublins be coming?"

"Mercy on us! Look at that long gentleman! He's as good as a corpse already."

The recipient of this shaft, not being an Irishman, gave a sickly smile, as his men tittered and hurled back retorts into the welter. The women were fierce and tearful. One escaped the constable, and, rushing up to an officer, lifted an imploring face to his.

"Bring him back safe, misther; bring him back safe! He's the only one I have, and a good boy;" then, changing to a cheerful scream—"Kill the murtherers; kill them, and bring me back a helmet."

So, for a brief moment they were the heroes of their womenkind, and crammed full of glorious thoughts that disappeared hurriedly at the irritated voice of the embarkation officer—

"What are your men standing about there for? Bring them along, man, if you want to get away tonight. You're only going to England. There'll be time enough for goodbyes. Get a move on!"

And the company learned the most elementary fact in modern war, that heroics have a proper place and time. It is pleasant to think of your future gallantry and pat yourself on the back because you are going to be a fine fellow, but, if you do, your Fighting Strength Return will inevitably be late. Still, on the chilly crossing as they looked back on those elementary days in the workhouse at Mallow, at those night schemes, at the hard, fine days at Fermoy, with the packed cinema and lazy evenings on the river, and the great billiard matches and the indiscreeter delights of " the Roche"—muddled, interflowing thoughts of pleasure and duty—they felt that they were entering the last phase before they "went out."

2. The Months Before

It is not generally known that the body-belt is an effective instrument of prophecy. Soon after arrival at Pirbright, they indented for "belts, body," and were told that they would be supplied immediately before proceeding overseas. The history, then, of the months before going out was a history of gradual equipment, culminating in body belts. Twice a week the quartermaster-sergeant went down to the Field Stores and was given anything from rifles to pantaloons, cook's cart to coaster hubs. Twice a week when he returned, we asked a question.

There were rumours, of course. We were going post-haste to the Dardanelles. Salonica was crying for us. Irishmen never fought so well as they had to fight in East Africa. A raid on Schleswig was contemplated, and everybody knew that the Danes were particularly fond of Irishmen. General Joffre had earnestly requested that the Irish Division might be sent to fight side by side with his brave fellows in the Vosges. Irishmen, when they had seen them, had always been enthusiastic about the Vosges.

The orderly-room sergeant had it on unimpeachable authority that January 22 was the date. These dates, he said loftily, were of course arranged months beforehand for the benefit of the Navy, or so as not to interfere with trade. All these rumours we treated with the credulity they deserved. Stoutly maintaining in the mess that they were worthless, it was pointed out to the more sceptical that there is no smoke without fire—and secretly believed. Yet very deep down in our hearts we trusted in the body-belts alone. When they really had come, the great measles scare tested our faith. Schnapps, sitting on the edge of his bed, held his auburn head in his hands and groaned aloud—

"And to think that after all these months we should be held back because the Munsters have a case or two of measles!"

But, as you will hear, body-belts triumphed even over measles.

During these last days the Fairy Godmother lavished her utmost. We had arrived in England with a few old rifles, some ancient cycles, and little else. When first the flow of presents began everybody was tremendously excited.

"Have you heard that the new vests have come?"

"Yes, and they say our field stationery box is due tomorrow."

Then we grew more careless, yet insisted more on smartness, and felt a little more soldierly. The disreputable cyclists gradually came to be modern soldiers, workmanlike beings hideously attired and compassed about with so many implements and fancies that they jingled and swung—like those harassed men who march bravely along the street playing five instruments at once.

During these "months before" polish was vigorously applied. First there was Platoon Training, when Peter, riding upright with low saddle and high handle-bars, would pedal rapidly into the distance with his men in perfect interval behind him. No one quite knew where he went. Chobham and Worplesdon must have echoed to his emphatic and many-tongued advice.

Then punctually to the moment Peter would reappear, pedalling unconcernedly at the same even, rapid pace (uphill or downhill it never varied), and his men, keeping an even more perfect interval, would have a far-away look in their eyes and be murmuring certain new phrases for private use.

Then came Company Training, when our Bill would be set to stem the company's advance, or when, spread over a wide front, the platoon commanders would endeavour to keep touch by an eternal succession of messages. Everybody always claimed to have captured everybody else, so everybody returned cheered.

The two great days were those on which the Company took

the field against the myriad cyclists of the Training Centre. Will Fitz's platoon ever forget how they held a bridge for the morning, and then, when ordered to retire, were pursued at top speed through the streets of Old Woking—how Fitz, barely a hundred yards in front, dashed up a byroad, and, turning, shot down the enemy as they passed? And that same day our Bill laid a neat little double ambush and collared a platoon.

The Training Centre had its revenge, a foul, misty night. With a Hunnish subtlety they defended themselves with grenades, and the Irish cyclists, indignant at this reception, retaliated fiercely until they were outnumbered. Cuts and black eyes called for revenge. The Gaspipe took counsel with Bill the Bomber, and prepared sundry explosive devices against a second night. And the attack, carefully planned, never came off, because, though Peter led his platoon secretly along an undiscovered path, the reserve platoon got hopelessly lost.

That was the first night of service conditions. The Gaspipe had ordered Cicero to find a headquarters in Chobham, and Cicero, with a skill he has since maintained, found a charming, discreetly-furnished little house, warm and comfortable, where the Gaspipe, after an excellent dinner, wove plans at his ease for the destruction of the enemy.

One afternoon the Gaspipe sent Cicero to Ockham to find a billet for the company, which came to Ripley late in the evening. At last they reached the farm prepared, made a huge fire, and slept through a freezing night in barns and lofts. It was horribly realistic to wake up in the night with frozen toes and wriggle desperately trying to find out whether it is better to put the hardest or the softest part of oneself next the boards.

Towards the end of the third month certain definite signs appeared that put anxious joy into the company's heart. The body-belts were promised at an early date. Musketry was nearly finished and inspections had begun.

There was that first inspection when a certain C.O., not hearing the bugle, found himself saluting nothing in particular by himself. The inspecting general galloped round and, when immediately behind the Gaspipe's back, started putting questions—a situation that demanded consummate and gymnastic tact. Should the Gaspipe turn, his cycle would be certain to strike some horse's leg. Should he look straight to his front, his soldierly answer would be lost in the wind. So, in a spirit of compromise he turned his head, and, looking upwards, as one looks at a second-storey window, he replied.

The march past, too, had its difficulties. Cyclists march past in lines, and officers, of course, salute with the right hand, looking the inspecting general full in the face. The cycle, which is on the right, must therefore be pushed by the left hand. Let the uninitiated experiment. Push a cycle with the left hand on the right side, while saluting with the right hand and gazing fixedly to the right—this on a sheet of the slipperiest mud with a strenuous endeavour to keep a straight course. The usual result is that the cycle slips farther and farther away, so that, unless a rapid recovery be made immediately after passing the saluting-point, a regrettable incident is bound to occur.

Then came the Queen's Parade—when, Nationalist and Unionist, we all cheered Her Majesty as lustily as we could—though distinctly out of time, because the attendant aeroplanes made so much noise that we on the right of the line could not hear what was going on. The Gaspipe glanced to the left and saw the staff waving vigorously and silently. For a moment he was too shy to start cheering on his own, so the cyclists were a little late. . . .

Sundry problems vexed our last weeks—the problem of "Love Marriage." The Gaspipe longed for that delightful counsellor, Miss Annie Swan, to come to his aid. Marriage and Birth and Leave were unfortunately related. The Gaspipe would be sitting by the fire with a comfortable pipe when M'Gee, the mess-waiter, would come in, and after doing nothing in particular for a long while, at last approach, standing sternly at attention.

"Well, M'Gee, what do you want?"

M'Gee blushed and choked.

"I'm afther getting married, sorr."

"Well?"

"I'm wondering if I could be getting leave, sorr."

"All right, M'Gee. I've no objection to marriage in general or yours in particular. When do you want to go?"

"On Wednesday, sorr. We'll be getting married that day."

"Don't you want to go before to make arrangements?"

"No, sorr. The young lady says she would prefer to make them herself."

"All right; you can go. But bring back a certificate, and don't be late."

The certificate had to be produced, because a word in favour of marriage that the Gaspipe had let drop produced a host of applications. When certificates were demanded, the number dropped but was still high. He was not sure whether marriage was endured because of the leave, or leave requested because of the marriage. One lad was heard to remark judiciously—

"On the whole, it's worth it."

But when a man put in two applications for marriage-leave within three months, and a leave to be present at the birth of his first-born a few weeks later . . . Leave for births required as careful discrimination. Finally, there was the adventurer who, in an access of probably assumed and certainly confused emotion, asked in grief-stricken tones—

"For leave, sorr, to wrong the young leddy that I've righted."

The second problem was that of battle-wear. A discreet compromise had to be struck between smartness and safety. Our pioneer battalion appeared one morning in "battle-tunics" that suggested the potential airman with a dash of old-fashioned gunner. Like the advertisements, they were "different," and undoubtedly practical. Should the cyclists also wear high collars and remove their badges of rank to the inconspicuous, sober shoulder-strap? Should they wear *putties* or gaiters or field boots? It was a hard problem, but spiced deliciously with the excitement of impending danger. They pictured the Hun lying in wait and murmuring to himself—

"Ah, that is an officer. I will shoot him!"

They saw the Hun inevitably missing, and themselves dashing forward to complete his capture. Still, it was scarcely wise to give the fellow even a chance. Some, however, contended that whatever the battle-wear, the Hun would perceive in their grace of bearing and attitude of command the symbols of their rank. George settled the question by remarking drily—

"If you're frightened of showing your necks, turn up your collars and use safety-pins."

One fine day the body-belts arrived, and the company was speechless with joy. The Gaspipe consumed his last Christmas dinner. A farewell concert was given, with a dance, for which a number of seemly damsels were brought from the neighbouring town and sent home under the eager escort of Cicero in a motor-bus. Kit was hastily gone through, and deficiencies made good. But still the order did not come.

And there was one bitter circumstance that blunted our happy excitement. Peter was claimed by the Ministry of Munitions. He could have refused, but a man who can organise a factory is more important than a man who can organise a platoon. With a cultured cruelty Peter was not taken at once, but was left to wander round aimlessly on the night of our departure, a lost and blasphemous soul. That is why in the future records of the Irish cyclists you will read not of Peter but of Samuel, who came in his place.

There is a hope that, when Peter has finished his job, when the factory has been organised so that the machines run as smoothly as his platoon and the girls work as strenuously as his men, Peter will return to us. Then once again will our fervent objurgations fall lifeless to the ground, pale by the side of his richly coloured phrases.

3. Going Out

One morning the Gaspipe was sitting as usual in his office with his neatly piled papers before him. On the walls were pinned plans and parade states and a list of those returns which, whatever betide, must be punctually and accurately sent in. Corporal Carmody sat opposite, composing laboriously one of those many documents that a company is supposed to hand out to embarkation officers, landing officers, transport officers, and all the other officers that carefully pilot a unit overseas. A despatch-rider, half hidden by an enormous revolver, dashed in. He looked very important.

Perhaps, like all good despatch-riders, he knew the contents of every despatch he carried. The despatch was secret. Faintly hoping—there had been so many false alarms—the Gaspipe tore open the second envelope. He read the message, gave a receipt, and, when the despatch-rider had disappeared, turned to his faithful clerk—

"Carmody, we're going immediately!"

The clerk turned a lusty red and choked out—

"Oh, sir!"

It was not a remarkable answer, but it was expressive. It contained all the mad desire of the Irish Division, which had been so long training and so wearily, to get out—to get out to the Front at any cost.

A rough rumour of the despatch's contents flew round the camp, and the preparations that were made turned rumour into likely truth. Fitz was all laughter. George smiled grimly. The

Child shrieked with joy; and Schnapps? If I could describe to you the face of Schnapps, I should be describing all the wild delight that has ever been seen. . . .

The last night came. We played a little bridge, and talked and pretended that, after all, going to the Front was a very ordinary matter. The *padre* came in to say goodbye, and we proudly thanked him for his kind wishes. And Peter, utterly disconsolate, wandered from one room to another and did little useful things.

At midnight we banqueted off sausages and toast and tea. Then the officers, wearing all their equipment, went out on parade to their waiting men. The Gaspipe, collecting the last oddments, followed. The men stood eagerly in the darkness. Some of those who were being left behind clung enviously to the edge of the parade-ground.

"Goodbye, Peter. Are we all ready now, Cicero? Right. Advance in file—from the right of platoons. Headquarters leading!!"—and they moved off into a steady tramp, singing a few songs.

When they came to the station there was old Harry Tatton, one of the rejected, down on some excuse to see them off. Finally, they were entrained, and at last—after an age, it seemed—the train slid out of the station, and poor old Harry was left shouting on the platform. So the Irish cyclists started overseas. . . .

Now, if an account of this journey were to be written from the instructions that preceded it, the chronicler would describe how the Gaspipe at every stop handed out returns to the dignified staff, how the company on detraining or disembarking formed itself glibly into little parties, each knowing its own job. Unfortunately, the war has dealt sadly by many instructions.

The train steamed in alongside an immense covered platform, and a one-armed Australian took charge—

"No, thanks. I don't want that particular return—it's washed out. Get fifty men and have these waggons off. Put the rest of the men over there. You've got a party specially told off to unload? Never mind, anybody can get a waggon off. Come along with the nearest fifty men."

Jumping on to the truck, he started to cast off the lashings himself. The Gaspipe sighed at the thought of his carefully organised parties, but, with the skilful Australian to pull and push and untie and direct, the train was cleared in no time at all. Then after the Gaspipe had signed papers the Australian made tea, and over the cake talked about Gallipoli, and of how, when he had recovered from his wound, he had importuned everybody he knew for a job.

All day they were kept at the docks. Then, as it grew dusk, they were marched on board the transport. The Gaspipe, remembering the time when he had spent the coldest of nights on some coils of rope, looked round his cabin with delight. After supper he turned in.

In the middle of the night his head collided with something violently. The ship seemed to be moving in all directions at once. George lay utterly miserable. On deck the guard hung limply over the rail, wished for a submarine or anything to take away his attention from that burning problem. . . .

Feeble but happy, they landed in the morning and marched through the warehouses to another quay. What pure delight it was to be told to keep to the right! The French air too, had a different smell. It would have all been wonderfully exciting if they could only have got rid of that queasy feeling in the stomach.

They spent the morning unloading their bicycles and transport, and then braced themselves to ride over that *pavé* which the Gaspipe had described to them so vividly. He had said that it required months of daily practice to ride well on greasy *pavé*. He, of course, had had that practice—in fact, had never "come off" a bicycle in his life, but he fully expected them to be all over the road at the start. Very gingerly they mounted. They had scarcely ridden a hundred yards when the second platoon heard a dull crash in front and a muttered oath. They rode on and saw the Gaspipe standing indignant by the wayside pathetically testing an injured knee. . . .

In the afternoon the Gaspipe went in search of some old friends. There was the station which he had searched so feverishly for his Company, and the street in which he had left his useless bicycle. Along that road were the Wool Warehouses where they had slept with fleas, or on the stones the night before they entrained for Landrecies.

The girls did not come now with garlands in adoration. The town was not humming with rumours of an immediate victory. The small boys did not stand and gaze in wonder. Perhaps the indifference was due to the winter weather for now the boys came pestering with English magazines, the barber thought there was nothing in this rumoured German offensive, and the girls, instead of flowers, brought collecting-boxes. Would the kind officer spare a *sou* for the children of those who had fallen in defence of their country?

The zest of war had hastened away.

Yet, just as those despatch-riders—Fat Boy and Huggie and Grimers and Boo and the rest of them had stood waiting in fatigued excitement at Point Six: Hangar de Laine, so Fitz and Schnapps and George stood now with their men waiting. The Irish cyclists were entraining at Point Quatre, where the 2nd Cavalry Brigade entrained in the first August of the war. Things had changed a little. In entraining and detraining there are always long hours of waiting. The despatch-riders shivered hungry in the cold, but the Irish cyclists filed past a canteen, where the most charming of ladies, with a little aid from Schnapps, dispensed hot tea and cocoa and cakes with an untiring patience.

The canteen was a godsend. It is good to drink a scalding cup of coffee off the bar at the bottom of Oakley Street in the dark hours of the morning, to dine late at Milan while waiting for the Riviera Express, to take coffee and rolls at Pontarlier or Bale or Flushing, to breakfast at leisure on the Irish Mail or at Covent Garden, when all wise people are in bed; but nothing is better for a soldier than to find a canteen on his cold, uncomfortable, and infinitely tiring journey.

We rumbled out an hour before daybreak, and slept a little, though it was very cold. Early in the morning we stopped and found another canteen, at which we made our breakfast. The inevitable occurred. Cicero, awakened from a heavy slumber, was late in buying his cakes. The train started, and Cicero, hearing shouts, rushed out to find it moving slowly past him. At this moment of crisis, he showed his greatness. A lesser man, in an agony at the thought of being left behind, would have jumped on the nearest waggon.

But Cicero, with a bottle of hot coffee in one hand and cakes in his pocket, solemnly pounded after the train. His face was very serious, and his fierce auburn moustaches bristled with determination. Cicero and his carriage reached the end of the platform at the same moment. For a second there was breathless suspense. Then, still grasping the bottle like an inveterate old tippler, he was hauled in triumphantly. . . .

Late in the afternoon we came to Abbeville. The Gaspipe made a dash for the square. When last he had seen it, the square had been crammed full of troops and of transport in preparation for that forced march which brought us opposite La Bassée, on the left of the French. Now it was empty, save for one or two Indian troopers.

In the gathering dusk we trundled north—past the Hospital of the Duchess, past Boulogne, and on. We stopped again. Instructions and a map were handed in. So, we knew at last to which sector of the line we were going. There was no more sleep. Eagerly we discussed our prospects, and papers were searched for the latest news. The train proceeded very slowly, and stopped again and again.

Finally, a corporal of police put his head in at the window. He was to be our guide, and we questioned him in a furious desire for knowledge. How many miles were we from the firing line? Were things going well? What divisions were here? Had the rest of the division arrived?

The company unloaded in the ochreous light of great flares. Rations and kit were piled on the waggons. The Irish cyclists filed out of the station and then started after their guide. They came to the crest of a rise that overlooked the country to the east. Far away there was a little flash, just like the flashes in the air that the trains make on the District Railway. Then, after a long interval, came a little low threatening murmur. And somebody behind the Gaspipe said slowly, in a tone of deep reverence

"The guns"

4. Back Again

1

You have read how, for many soul destroying months, the Irish cyclists prepared; how at last the Channel was crossed in a lively gale; how after certain adventures they detrained one wet night ten miles from the nearest Boche; and how, struggling to the top of a rise against a testy head-wind and a flurry of rain, they saw the lights of the line and heard the guns.

Away from the hissing flares, the banging of the trucks, the long-winded shrieks of the French engines, the weary shouted orders, the mixed smell of horses and stale food and wet coal; from all the cheerful but hurried uproar of the station, it was dark on the road and lonely. They did not know whether the guns were near or far.

Sentries, their shoulders covered with shining capes or waterproof sheets, stepped out from nowhere and challenged mysteriously. Their guide, too, hesitated, and once turned back, saying the road was dangerous. The tired men thought that this black night they might be led along perilous tracks fringed with sniper-ridden trees. The youngest officer dared not strike a match for fear some Hun should take a more careful aim. It was the Front.

If the Gaspipe had realised how they felt and had seen fit for the moment to stop explaining to the guide the character and ultimate abode of guides, he might have pointed out that even in the bad old days Fritz had never penetrated ten miles behind our lines. But the Gaspipe was longing for billets and the day.

The guide, a sergeant in that stubborn corps the military police, had murmured at the station how exceedingly lucky it was that he and not an interpreter was to lead. He knew the country like a book, day or night, wet or fine.

"We don't want to see all the country," it was urged; "not all of it only just that little bit on either side of the most direct road to our billets."

But the guide was an errant humourist. He led them along nightmare and roundabout roads, protesting that he used to cycle a bit as a boy himself, and that all other roads were dangerous. Finally, when he trotted gallantly into a village suspiciously like a village, they had ridden through half an hour or so before, he remarked with a horrid laugh that the longest way round was the shortest way home.

At four in the morning a feeble and dispersed column of soaked and weary cyclists, led by a maddened officer and a subdued guide, halted outside a mean and filthy little village. An apologetic interpreter came to meet them with the news that billets had been carefully arranged for a third of their company. The remaining billets were occupied. The Gaspipe looked at the sticky mud on the uneven cobbles and at the shabby farms. He smelt the smell, then discovering the truth from the interpreter, said joyously—

"This is indeed France. Where is the *estaminet?*"

Some sort of shelter was found for all the men. The officers crowded into an *estaminet,* where a weary little dark woman, without a word of complaint, bustled round and made them steaming hot coffee, cut them bread-and-butter, and showed them where they could sleep. . . .

They rose late, ashamed of the night's fears and eager for bold adventures; but the village at first chilled them. Surrounded by fields of black mud, the dirty little houses, for the most part almost farms, irregularly fringed a narrow street of *pavé*, slippery with evil grease. The rickety barns were filled with the effluvia of drying clothes, ordure, tinned stuff, stale cooked food, and rifle oil. The dripping midden heaps, subdued by the slow, persistent rain, thickened and poisoned the air.

From the kitchens escaped the faint blue smoke and everlasting odour of frying fat. The dingy *estaminets* were like empty glasses of bad beer into which worse coffee had been poured. All the roads from the village were streaming and polluted and covered with a smear of viscous mud. December in the country behind the Loos salient is never pleasant, and Houchin is the dismallest village that ever was.

But the Irishmen were singing and laughing with the excitement they could not suppress; and when the general walked in to tell them that his car was stuck a mile away, the cheeriest party set out to dig under it and drag it out with ropes.

Then word came that they were to move up nearer to the line, in order to repair some old trenches. There were shouts of joy. Nearer the line was nearer the line to them, even if to the initiated work on third or fourth line trenches does not appear to hold the elements of hilarious or romantic fighting.

So, the next morning they started off, and halting to verify the road, watched pass a battalion of infantry from the trenches—infinitely weary but half smiling men, wholly covered with mud and chalk. Some had bound sackcloth round their legs to above their knees, some were limping quickly in a desperate effort to keep up—all looked strained and beaten about. It was the cyclists' first sight of war.

Finally, they came to a large group of mine buildings, and Cicero was sent to see the *corons*, or workmen's cottages, in which the company had been ordered to billet. Of course, they were full; but with tact and energy cover was found for the men in the lamp room, the engine-room, attics, and tents.

2.

An officer once told me he had refused an interesting, well paid job at the Base, because he "wanted to see it through, and could not leave it now." The cynic will say he was not in the infantry. True, for he commanded one of those odd units that lately-arrived infantry subalterns, who do not understand, are inclined to treat with condescension and envy. The man did not want to see it through because he had been comfortable and safe.

In the unbearable first winter of the war he had existed for forty days in the first line without once going down a communication trench; held a 300 yards' gap with two machine guns and no ammunition; lived for days together on casualties' packs and water that was nothing but distilled essence of dead men. He had been through these noisome, incredible months, the like of which we shall never see again, when we had nothing except endurance, and the German everything except victory.

First, there is the fascination of the game. Old hands who have seen the drama unfold cannot go away until the curtain has been rung down, in case they should be called upon to play again a part upon the stage. The story of the great marches, the early open battles, the holding of a tenuous line against overwhelming numbers and skill and ammunition, the desperate futile attempts at premature offensives, the pouring of shells and men into the country, the slow but remorseless change from inferiority to equality, and from equality to the definite fact of being superior to the enemy in everything that counts, the industrious preparations for the first of the big successful attacks, the launching of it, and the sagging and cracking of the whole German line—that is a story which must thrill and amaze those who *read* its chapters. Think of the old hands who have not read but taken part. Can you wonder that they want to see it through?

Then some of us have a curious perverted affection for the forlorn country from Loos to Ypres. Down south we have not seen and do not know. It is the line from Loos to the north that holds memories. In Maroc, that red brick wilderness of shattered villas and workmen's cottages, with their hidden mysteries and broken, sprawling mines and factories and rectangular overgrown gardens—do you remember, Schnapps, how the Gaspipe came through squalid Les Brebis on a sunny morning, how he climbed up the rickety ladder to look at the Hun, then walked along the rural trenches from which you can see the sinister

Double Grassier, the great rusty belt of German wire sidling up the hill to the craters above Loos, the peaceful village and huge tangled metalwork of the mine buildings?

We have gazed very often at the little city of vermilion roofs, the three gaunt elevators, and the big shining white tower of the Metallurgique. And the trenches—the dismal stretch of sodden, bloodstained, roughly piled sand-bags west of the Sunken Road—or when we went looking at the fire steps in front of the Chalk Pit Wood or behind the Hulluch craters? Go north of the canal. It is something to have been in Violaines, to have seen Givenchy and Festubert and Richebourg St Vaast before they were touched by shells. Now you must look carefully in the rank grass for the foundations of the *estaminets* that two years ago were brigade headquarters.

Those officers who sometimes enter Bethune may try and imagine the morning on which the inhabitants turned out to watch curiously the first English troops they had seen press hurriedly through to secure the left flank of the French. Farther north, it is a long time since a brigade selected Cockshy House, not far from Laventie, and found the Germans had stolen the spoons; since the first shell startled Neuve Eglise; since that abominable bit of road near Dranoutre was repaired; since French headquarters were at Dickebusch; since we went looking for a piano in the *château* at Vormezeele; since cocktails were sold in Ypres; since we used to think Poperinghe the safest place in the world, and go for tea to that best of *pâtisseries*; since the Boche experimented with gas-shells on the *château* at Boesinghe.

It is good to go back to these towns and villages and inns even in their desolation. It would be better to return, as we shall, to that cake-shop at St Quentin and the view of Mons from above Athis. . . .

Sometime in the distance, when by the mint-beds of the Windrush you wander lazily and dream a vague dream of the old dim war, you will see and understand what now would surely repel any man—the sights and sounds and smells of the country behind the Line. The long straight roads with battalions marching, and the strings of lorries with the smell they leave behind of petrol, hot grease, and dust; the dilapidated little French carts, the dainty motor ambulances, and the old men in blue tunics and steel helmets slowly repairing. You will remember how you wondered whether you ought to salute that car—there was a flash of red. Then the towns swarm with mess carts, and limbers, and officers on horseback, and any number of odd, aimless men.

The stuffy, brightly-lighted *coiffeur* is always crowded, and ruled imperiously by *Madame's* harsh voice. Officers are carrying bottles and tins and boxes from the canteen to their limbers or carts. Farther forward all the billets are numbered and ticketed. It is a cold wet evening, and the men, who a moment ago marched in singing, are wearily tramping round in small groups under their corporals looking for the barns or the sheds where they have been told to sleep. . . . The villages are full of lazy, lounging men, resting or in reserve.

You will not have forgotten all the little notices: "Washing for officers and soldiers" "Eggs, chips, beer"—"English beer"—"Teas, eggs, butter, chips"—"Officers' Tea Rooms"; mingled with "D.A.D.O.S."—"C.R.E."—"C. Mess"—"Pioneer Stores," and all the rest of them. Off the muddy roads are always parked transport and horse-standings, stout but flimsy-looking sheds, with the muddiest cart tracks in the world.

Farther forward still are the shattered villages. Innumerable wires fringe and cross every road and track. Hidden batteries appear in odd places, and great heaps of wire and timber, bombs, and stores miscellaneous are scattered everywhere. Little graveyards and odd graves lie serenely by the roadside. Then in a rough country lane or in the middle of some collapsed mine buildings, you came to a newly-painted board—"SOUTHERN UP." You used to enter the trench here, walking carefully on the slippery boards and smelling that deathly earthy smell, and so to that trench, which is like all other trenches except that sentries are looking through periscopes.

Such a catalogue of facts must fail. What you remember of the sights and smells is perhaps the swollen, green body of the fellow who was gassed, or the acrid fume and dull near thuds when you walked down a communication trench between batteries that were firing "gunfire five seconds," or the stench of frying fat and stale coffee in the kitchen of your billet, or the rush and clear singing of little bits, the thumps of flying clods, the scream, the curse, and the cold, queasy feeling in the stomach when the Boche opened on your trench. But perhaps even a catalogue can help those to understand why some want to live it through. . . . And in Flanders, mud, rain, and cheerless weather are looked for, because fine weather in Flanders is a strange state of affairs. . .

5. Odd Jobs: And Some Minor Arts

1

Cyclists in France have a past and a future but no very glorious present. They look back with longing at those great days when they held on for that extra quarter of an hour to cover the retreat of the division's rearguard, or when, advancing, they pedalled merrily ahead, rounding up all the odd Boches who might lurk behind hedges and in farms, to the confusion of the blind infantry, and occasionally engaging in cheery little actions with obstinate rearguards. The cyclists then were like terriers, snuffing round in the highest spirits. One day, the cyclists tell you, the Boche line will break.

Only the ignorant infantry, with their parochial ideas on the eternity of trench warfare, believe that peace will be declared with the Germans at La Bassée. Great, disconnected armies will retire eastward sullenly, or perhaps the enemy will go back to a second line for a start, leaving rearguards. . . . Then the terriers will come into their own again, snuffing, biting, and yapping at Fritz's dignified heels, smelling out machine-guns and mined roads, drawing woods, clearing farmsteads.

Infantry think in yards, cyclists in miles. If ever the infantry are to advance in column of route, somebody must see that the long column does not find itself in company that it would prefer to meet in quite another formation.

Meanwhile there are odd jobs to be done, all sorts of odd jobs, some in the front line and some behind it. The cyclists must keep fit for the day.

Perhaps infantry may read what I write. So, let me write this. The cyclists may do now those little jobs for which you have no time or men. They may not now "go over the top" or spend all their time in the trenches though some battalions must remember how a few platoons of stout, cheery, and always willing men came to give them a hand but let the infantry never forget that without the cyclists the Great Retreat would have been a blacker nightmare than it was, that without the cyclists the Great Advance would have been less rapid than it was, that in October of '14 it was the cyclists who rallied the infantry when the Germans broke through at Violaines.

So, every morning Fitz, the Babe, or another pushed along the *pavé* into Noeux-les Mines, between the slag heaps, to Mazingarbe, and on to those curious out-of-the-way places where second and third line defences run, or along the railway track to the bumpiest of all roads, or through mean Sailly-Labourse. They stacked their cycles neatly by the roadside, marched across clinging plough to some rakish old trenches, and set to work building up traverses, resurrecting fire steps, exhuming dug-outs, thickening parapets, until the trenches looked no longer rakish but neat and good and new, even if laid out on rather an old-fashioned plan. Expert advice and untruthful information were provided copiously and for nothing by a sapper sergeant.

It was all novel and tremendously exciting—and occasionally shells did come their way. One night the Babe returned with a tale of how a big shell had exploded just off the road, covering them with mud. A solitary shell is just a solitary shell, but to this band of Irish warriors it was the beginning of a new life: it was the reason for those weary months at Mallow, Ballyvonare, Ballyhooly, Fermoy, and Pirbright. . . .

The Gaspipe going his rounds would find Fitz and Bill in pipes and shirt-sleeves remaking with deliberate care a model bay, Cicero would be holding forth on the theory of revetting, or George, looking very chilly, would be marching stern-eyed up and down outside the trench. Brady D., the wit of the company, leaning gracefully on a spade, with his sallies would be encouraging the others to work before going off to find an abandoned dug-out in which to read a pink paper at his ease.

Just in front were two big guns. Some days the gunners would fire them, but every day two servants under the eloquent and enthusiastic instruction of the colonel were planting things that never grew. I went back a year later to see.

Three miles away against the sky were the houses of Maroc on a slight ridge that, crossed by the Lens road, stretched away to the northward. The ridge was covered with a delicate tracery of white lines—the rearward chalk trenches of the salient. Between the slope and the working Irishmen was a big mining village, often shelled, dominated by a black pyramid of a slag heap. If you examine that white tracery of used and disused trenches carefully you will see that one line runs parallel with the crest of the ridge and just below it. That is the old German line.

Two or three hundred yards nearer is another line, the old British line. You are looking at the battlefield of Loos, for Loos itself and the Chalk Pit Wood are in the valley beyond the ridge, while the next slope is Hill 70. Or again walk out in front of the big mining village and turn to your left. That low black squat thing is the monstrous Dump, those earthworks the Hohenzollern Redoubt, and far away, glistening pink in the sun, is the shattered ruin of Givenchy church.

The Babe and his fellows had nothing yet to do with trenches. They only knew of them as dangerous places to be avoided. But lest your appetite should have been whetted by the sight of the rearward trenches of the Line, later I will take you through those trenches and tell you all about a battle, of which you probably know nothing, fought on the field of Loos.

2

Repairing old trenches, with a shell or two dropping near every few days, is a gentle introduction to the lesser arts of war. The Irishmen learnt that the report of a gun and the explosion of a shell, though both loud, are not necessarily similar—that if you stop your work to watch the "Archies" the work will take a long time to do—that sappers are not always truthful. They began to know the different kinds of gun by sight and by noise. Soon they were finding their way with tolerable ease amongst that complex organisation which lies hidden in ruined houses and *châteaux* and mine buildings. They started to read the *communiqués* with eagerness and discuss them with an expert knowledge.

They brought back from quartermaster's stores and other such temples of truth the most incredible and fantastic rumours. They were fed to satiety with stories of the Battle of Loos, which had scarcely finished its ugly course when the Irishmen arrived in France. Soon the gloss of newness was replaced by a veteran roughness and understanding.

Never look as if you were going to fight, is the warning for the novice. A revolver is carried only in the front line trenches, and not always there. Staff officers stroll round the trenches wearing an immaculate Sam Browne devoid of military ornament. That is the fault of stationary warfare. In some safe and pleasant mansion, the G. S.O.I, of a division enjoys an excellent lunch and smokes a good cigar. The car comes round at half-past two. At half past six he returns, and an hour later sits down to a dinner even more excellent than his lunch.

Yet between dinner and lunch the G.S.O.I. may have been within 100 yards or so of the Boche. Why carry a revolver? The chance that you will meet a German while you are taking a laborious walk round the trenches is microscopic. You require only a stick, a gas helmet, a steel helmet, and a small flask.

The history of steel helmets differs from that of revolvers. If an officer were to spend a few days or nights walking from one end of an army front to the other, it would be the most consummate good fortune if he met a German, but he would be quite certain to meet a number of shells, grenades, Minnies, and bullets sufficient to test his helmet.

Yet, unlike the French, whose *paveurs*, or road-menders, are equipped with picturesque *casques*, the "tin hat" is rarely worn except when in, going to, or coming from the trenches. It is a protection useful in certain localities, not a universal article of attire. The old days, when officers wore something because it was comfortable and efficient, are gone.

Immediately you leave a communication trench you must be neat and smart and like everybody else. There are still exceptions. Robinson, a brigade-major, used in the Somme to stroll up to his Advanced Brigade Headquarters in slacks, carrying habitually a few bottles, just as, a year and a half ago, at Wulverghem, every man—be he guide, servant, or relief—used to carry up a piece of wood and a sandbag or two when he went to the trenches.

3

The cyclists were billeted in and near a large group of mine buildings. The officers lived in some streets of small workmen's cottages. Settling down, they all learnt to know a little of the people in the north of France and to respect them greatly. All the men have gone. Only women and grandfathers and boys remain. It is impossible for those at home to picture a country in which there are no men of fighting age left, for in France the net is cast very wide.

There are practically no exemptions at all—but the old men, the women, and the children still carry on. Doddering ancients turn from slippered fireside to guide a plough. Boys struggle desperately and successfully with sowing machines that were meant to be managed by two grown men. Labour is replaced by overtime. Everybody goes out into the fields when it is still dark; and riding home in the dusk, you can hear, even if you cannot see, the machines and the people working in the fields.

Remember, too, that a foreign if allied army has been billeted on the country since October of '14 without respite. We pay well, but soldiery, if no longer brutal and licentious, are thoughtless and a hindrance to those already unfairly handicapped.

The Irishmen found themselves at home. They were Catholic, and many of them workers on the land. They were welcomed by the kindly, cheerful old French priests—all the young French priests had been called up—and possessed, it would seem, a dim ancestral bond with their hosts. They made friends more quickly and more warmly than any English or Scottish soldiers. Before they had been a day in the place O'Keilly was helping to carry the water, Paddy had an eye to the children, and Mike with his arms on the fence was breathing sweet nothings to the laughing, working daughters.

The Gaspipe was billeted with Mme. Detrenne. There were two little clean bedrooms in the cottage, one for him and one for *Madame* and the four children. Downstairs, you went through the kitchen into a small parlour full of ornaments and wax flowers and photographs and certificates of the prowess of Corporal Detrenne, who it appeared had won many cross-country races and given abundant satisfaction to the authorities. *Madame* was a curt, energetic, middle sized blowsy woman; but the work of the house was done by Detrenne's sister. She was tall, finely built, with large eyes and a wealth of dull brown hair.

She lived in another cottage, but spent all her time tending the children, more particularly Robert, who, having reached the age of three, objected loudly to breeches between the hours of four and six, and could only be stopped by the big officer coming into the kitchen and flashing his electric torch. Robert would stare open mouthed, then chuckle delightedly and try to catch the beam of light. The women were overflowing with kindness. If they saw the officer looking cold, they would dash in to make a fire. If the lamp was burning ill, they would bring him multitudinous candles.

The only trouble was that once a week Detrenne's sister took a bath in the kitchen, an unusual custom that *Madame* never imitated. Then, if the Gaspipe wished to enter the parlour, used as an orderly-room, he would find the door barred. If there was no urgent reason why he should enter, he would smoke a philosophic pipe outside. If some army form or paper had to be found immediately, he went on knocking. Then, after an interval, Detrenne's sister would unbar the door and disappear upstairs for a moment in a flurry of draperies and dull brown hair.

The Gaspipe entered his orderly room and came out quickly, or shutting his door with a loud bang, enabled Venus to return to her bath.

One night, rather late, Fitz was in the parlour with the Gaspipe when a French soldier entered the kitchen. The Gaspipe was expecting the interpreter, so Fitz, who speaks wonderful French, went out, welcomed him, and taking his overcoat from him hung it up. Detrenne laughed, murmuring politely that so courteous were the English they hung up your own overcoat for you in your own house. Fitz came back with a blush, tactfully shutting the door. Now this is war time and the north of France, so there were no effusive shouts and gesticulations behind the door.

Detrenne and his wife greeted each other with the quiet affection that novelists so feelingly attach to the meeting of Jack, who has just come back from big game shooting and James Dickson, his father's friend, who persuaded him to try Nairobi instead of suicide. The *Nord* is very nearly as undemonstrative as the north of England, and patronises the *Midi* with the same contemptuous indulgence that your Lancashire lad uses towards the dull but flighty inhabitants of the south of England. . . .

In a few minutes the door was opened, and Detrenne came forward to ask us if we would do him the honour of sharing a bottle of wine. Fitz had to go, but the Gaspipe remained to sip the good red wine and talk of the war.

Detrenne was a quiet, bearded, wiry man of forty, holding the rank of adjutant in the infantry—a rank slightly higher than that of regimental sergeant-major. He had walked some twenty miles from the trenches near Arras, but did not seem tired. Although he had been in many battles from the Aisne onwards, he would not talk of his own exploits. His *Legion d'honneur?* It was a mere nothing! As *M. le Capitaine* would realise, one could not serve for so long without meeting "the chance." And if one did not take "the chance"—*pouf!*—it was one's own fault. If one did—well, one thanked the good God for the opportunity. No, he would prefer to talk of the big guns of the British.

The rumbling and the growling of the British big guns in the north was very cheering. When the wind came from the north and the thunder was more distinctly heard, they smiled at each other in the trenches, murmuring with a significance—*Les Anglais!* The British bomb was good too, but the *soixante-quinze* . . .! Yes, he had heard that 18-pdr. shrapnel was marvellously effective. . . . So, they talked into the small hours of the morning, while *Madame* sat quietly by with shining eyes, sometimes quietly interrupting with a word of explanation, sometimes endeavouring to force Detrenne to speak about himself, sometimes translating, because she was now acquainted with the vile accent of *M. le Capitaine.*

In the morning Detrenne put on an old coat and spent an hour or two pruning his favourite roses. Then he slipped down to the *estaminet*, while *Madame* remained at home working with Detrenne's sister, both cheerful, singing a little, and demurely proud when the neighbours came to call.

Eight days later Detrenne put on his greatcoat, took up his stick, quietly kissed his wife, and walked back to the trenches—twenty miles. . . . The children seemed a little fractious that evening, and, when the next night Mme. Dupont heard that her husband had been killed, *Madame* looked strained and anxious; but Detrenne's sister, who did most of the work, was as calm and unruffled as ever.

So the Irishmen learnt that if an officer takes the trouble to find out a little about the people amongst whom he is living; if he pays them the ordinary small courtesies of French life; if he realises that, though the women may seem a little extortionate in their charges, they are only trying to make their stewardship a success while the husband or the son is fighting; if, when the officer comes in to a billet in the evening he does not expect *Madame*, who during the day has done more than two men's work, to be in the sweetest of tempers—he will consider himself indeed lucky that the war has set him down among such honest, kindly, clever people. . . .

Jackson has lived for twenty months between Béthune and

Laventie. At four o'clock he returns from visiting his guns in the Line. *Maman* makes up the fire. Jackson takes off his boots. His socks are seen to be wet. She beseeches him to go and change them. *Papa* enters from the field. Jackson describes the trenches accurately but crudely. They all smile in sympathy. . . . After tea Jackson comes down into the kitchen, chaffing Adrienne, a fine handsome girl of seventeen, who counterattacks with vigour.

Julienne, the pretty, conceited little "flapper," who has come from La Gorgue to help with the potatoes, laughs self-consciously. Louis, the small boy who is doing a man's work in the fields, intervenes loudly, to be sternly squashed by *Papa*. Then they settle down, Adrienne to mending Jackson's socks. *Maman* stands, as always, with folded arms over the stove.

Julienne and Louis are grinning at each other. Jackson, who can do anything with his fingers, is sewing Louis' initials on to pillowcases, under the hilarious criticism of Adrienne, or discussing the contents of that excellent little paper, the *Télégramme*, with *Papa*. There are the old family jokes, "*Péronne n'est pas prise*," and exclamations of "*beaucoup peur*" when a gun is fired; full of resourceful humour is our M. le Commandant Jackson, and full of good tales and local gossip. He knows how Mme. Guyot, who has the big house over by La Vallée, is really a carpenter's daughter of Richebourg, although she always pretends she came from Paris.

He knows how Mme. Carette across the way hates officers' servants in her kitchen, and what Adele's brother is doing. He can tell you funny stories about M. Bogart, the cheerful wine-merchant of Laventie. He hates the Boche, as any northerner should, and sometimes, though his French is not Parisian (and all the better! What is Paris compared to the stout people of the Pas de Calais?), he brings out a word of *patois*, "*Ha, Adele, chinq* (pronounced "shank" = obviously "*cinq*") *sous pour la bière!*"

LEONAUR

ALSO FROM LEONAUR
AVAILABLE IN SOFTCOVER OR HARDCOVER WITH DUST JACKET

AFGHANISTAN: THE BELEAGUERED BRIGADE *by G. R. Gleig*—An Account of Sale's Brigade During the First Afghan War.

IN THE RANKS OF THE C. I. V *by Erskine Childers*—With the City Imperial Volunteer Battery (Honourable Artillery Company) in the Second Boer War.

THE BENGAL NATIVE ARMY *by F. G. Cardew*—An Invaluable Reference Resource.

THE 7TH (QUEEN'S OWN) HUSSARS: Volume 4—1688-1914 *by C. R. B. Barrett*—Uniforms, Equipment, Weapons, Traditions, the Services of Notable Officers and Men & the Appendices to All Volumes—Volume 4: 1688-1914.

THE SWORD OF THE CROWN *by Eric W. Sheppard*—A History of the British Army to 1914.

THE 7TH (QUEEN'S OWN) HUSSARS: Volume 3—1818-1914 *by C. R. B. Barrett*—On Campaign During the Canadian Rebellion, the Indian Mutiny, the Sudan, Matabeleland, Mashonaland and the Boer War Volume 3: 1818-1914.

THE KHARTOUM CAMPAIGN *by Bennet Burleigh*—A Special Correspondent's View of the Reconquest of the Sudan by British and Egyptian Forces under Kitchener—1898.

EL PUCHERO *by Richard McSherry*—The Letters of a Surgeon of Volunteers During Scott's Campaign of the American-Mexican War 1847-1848.

RIFLEMAN SAHIB *by E. Maude*—The Recollections of an Officer of the Bombay Rifles During the Southern Mahratta Campaign, Second Sikh War, Persian Campaign and Indian Mutiny.

THE KING'S HUSSAR *by Edwin Mole*—The Recollections of a 14th (King's) Hussar During the Victorian Era.

JOHN COMPANY'S CAVALRYMAN *by William Johnson*—The Experiences of a British Soldier in the Crimea, the Persian Campaign and the Indian Mutiny.

COLENSO & DURNFORD'S ZULU WAR *by Frances E. Colenso & Edward Durnford*—The first and possibly the most important history of the Zulu War.

U. S. DRAGOON *by Samuel E. Chamberlain*—Experiences in the Mexican War 1846-48 and on the South Western Frontier.